SOCIETY IN
REVOLUTIONARY
NORTH CAROLINA

SOCIETY IN REVOLUTIONARY NORTH CAROLINA

by

Alice Elaine Mathews

Raleigh 1976

TABLE OF CONTENTS

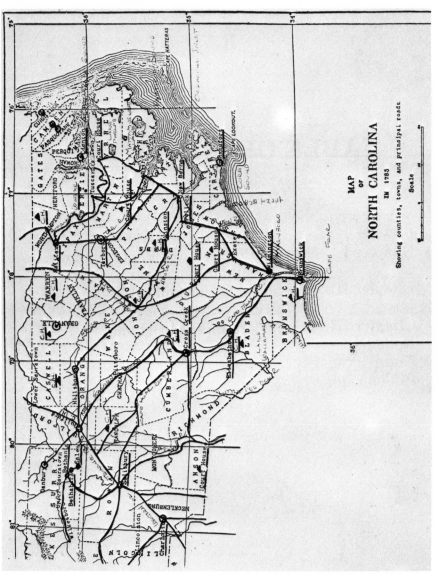

Map of North Carolina, 1783

PREFACE

North Carolina did not fall into the mainstream of the colonial South; that is, few men lived there who owned thousands of acres of land or who possessed numbers of slaves. The colony's (and later the state's) economic structure resembled much more the structure of the northern colonies than the other southern colonies. The typical North Carolinian was the small independent farmer — the yeoman freeholder — who lived modestly, hoped to acquire or maintain a comfortable living, was many times a religious dissenter, and, because of his isolation, was often very provincial. Yet the small farmers of North Carolina, despite their provincialism, put into practice American revolutionary theory — especially in their demand for responsible government.

A specific study of colonial and revolutionary society is lacking for the state, although textbooks of North Carolina history and regional studies generally devote one or two chapters to social conditions. Much more research is needed to understand North Carolina's social structure in the eighteenth century. What I have attempted to do in this pamphlet is to present an overall view of socioeconomic conditions in North Carolina during the Revolutionary Era and to make some suggestions about the structure of that society and to indicate some of its inner-tensions. I would especially like to thank my brother, Donald G. Mathews, and my colleagues, Max Williams and John Bell, for the suggestions that they made and my typist, Jeanne Nienhuis.

To be SOLD, at Public Sale,

On Thursday, the 19th March next,
At the Castle Inn, in the Town of
Suffolk,

By order of the Proprietor:

TEN likely NEGROES, confisting of men, women and children; a great variety of elegant and valuable Furniture, confisting of mahogany dining, card and Pembroke tables; mahogany and Windsor chairs, pier and dressing glasses, ten new goose feather beds, an elegant book-case, escrutoir and drawers, a billiard table, 30 pair of blankets, bed and table linen, China and glass ware, a library of books, together with many other articles of houshold and kitchen furniture; a horse and several cattle. The terms will be twelve months credit for all sums above five pounds, on giving bond with approved security to bear interest from the date if not punctually paid, a discount of ten per cent. will be allowed for ready payment in money, tobacco, or military certificates at their current value.

The above mentioned INN will be let on the same day, if not let before by private contract.

Suffolk, Feb. 10.   4

Notice of Slave Sale, 1789

CHAPTER I

NORTH CAROLINA IN THE REVOLUTIONARY ERA: A LAND OF OPPORTUNITY

"A young country is the fittest for a young man without a fortune," wrote young James Iredell from Edenton in 1772 to his invalid father in England. He would love to return home — to be near his family — but there his situation would be insecure, while in North Carolina he hoped, with "a tolerable certainty," to procure "in the course of a few years a genteel independency" — an income that would yearly provide him a comfortable living. Iredell was reading law under an excellent tutor and was clearly meeting the "Better Sort," who might help him to gain his "genteel independency." True, he missed his family; he suffered from the hot, humid summer days in Edenton; he had to watch his pennies carefully because of inflated prices. But he envisioned bright prospects. He had found a new home and new friends.[1]

While James Iredell was settling down to a life of comfortable respectability and a bright future — in part, guaranteed by his marriage to Miss Hannah Johnston — other individuals in the British Empire were not so fortunate. Three thousand miles away in the county of Sutherland in northern Scotland, a farmer nearly sixty years old was contemplating his family's prospects. He had lost many cattle "in the severe Winter 1771" and he was paying higher rents than his grandfather would ever have imagined (a 750 per cent increase). His two sons who were already settled in North Carolina kept urging him to migrate, and finally he made the fateful decision. It did not make much difference "in what Country he died," William Gordon told the customs officials in the spring of 1774, but by going to Carolina he hoped "that his children would earn their Bread more comfortably."[2] So they boarded the ship *Bachelor* bound for Wilmington in a land where the grass grew greener, the lushness of the forests and the fertility of the soil stirred the imagination and the cattle waxed fat; where one could obtain high wages quickly, buy land cheaply, and gain respectability. Revolutionary activities played no role in such visions.

North Carolina — the mention of its name in the 1760s and the 1770s meant abundance of provisions, cheap land, high wages; in short, a comfortable living to many immigrants, especially from the Scottish Highlands or the heavily populated colonies to the North. An anonymous writer, Scotus Americanus, noted in 1773 that North Carolina was "in its infancy, and newly settled" in comparison to its neighbors Virginia and South Carolina. "But, in the fertility of nature, Carolina has the advantage. In a word, the northern parts of it produce the same things with the southern parts of Virginia, and in greater perfection." On the other hand, "the southern parts of it produce the same things with which the northern parts of South Carolina abounds."[3] Not only Scotus Americanus, but his contemporaries as well as later writers have often compared North Carolina with her neighbors; and, although not all observers would reach the same favorable conclusions, they might agree with Scotus Americanus that North Carolina represented a unique position among the southern colonies; one that might very well encourage potential settlers.

One modern writer has remarked that "North Carolina was in some respects as much northern as southern," because of "the large middle class of small farmers" and "the relatively democratic distribution of wealth," even though it possessed traits "decisively southern," such as large plantations, slavery and an "almost exclusively rural character."[4] Of course, what was typically southern in the eighteenth century has never really been explained; but if a society dominated by a landholding aristocracy is meant, then North Carolina did not fit the pattern. It remained a small-white-farmer's paradise, where the industrious yeoman, the man with fifty acres of land or more, could have some voice in his destiny; a frontier society, in contrast to its colonial neighbors, where at least one Englishman (and probably more) found that too much of a leveling influence prevailed.[5] North Carolina's social order in many ways resembled more closely Virginia's in 1700 than Virginia's in 1770. Carolina was still in "a state of infancy," or, as a later adage put it: "North Carolina was the valley of humility between two mountains of conceit."

Despite her humble position, the colony possessed plentiful forests and fertile fields, which could easily be acquired. With a little labor, a plucky, hard-working individual could become a prosperous farmer and a respected member of the community. In such a place, what difference did his origins count or how he began in life? A French traveller in 1765 found the colony "a fine Country for poor people, but not for the rich." In fact, the Frenchman met very few rich people and noted that the fortunes of those that he did encounter consisted "generally in lands, which are for the most part uncultivated, and consequently of no advantage or value for the present." He believed that many of the new inhabitants were "convicts," (he probably meant indentured servants), who had served their time in Virginia and then had come south "where they are not known."[6] Many North Carolinians, indeed, did manage to keep their origins a well-kept secret — even to the present day.

Although aristocratic travellers, royal governors, even modern writers considered many of the new settlers poor, the latter did not perceive themselves as living in a state of poverty or at least staying in that condition once they had arrived in the promised land. If new arrivals did not have the money to purchase their first acreages, they had the choice of simply "squatting" on a piece of land as many did or working as day laborers until they had acquired enough savings to become men of property. A transplanted Marylander remembered that when his family first came to Orange County, "there were no poor laws nor paupers. Of the necessaries of life there were great plenty, but no luxuries." Or as Scotus Americanus noted a decade later: "poverty is almost an entire stranger" and added that "here a poor man need not fear the want of meat or employment."[7] A man might belong to the lower order, but in North Carolina he could acquire ample provisions, perhaps not luxuries, but enough to gain a comfortable, or what he considered a comfortable, living. What more did he need? Such prospects stirred the imagination.

On the eve of the Revolution North Carolina ranked fourth or fifth among the colonies in size of population and it was growing faster than any of the others. In the two decades between 1730 and 1750, the population doubled, but in the two decades between 1750 and 1770, the population nearly tripled — a factor primarily attributed to immigration. In 1766 Governor William Tryon wrote to the Board of Trade that "this province is settling faster than any on the continent" and added that "these inhabitants are a race of people differing in health and complexion from the natives in the maritime parts of the province; as much as a sturdy Briton differs from a puny Spaniard." Scotus Americanus, perhaps with a bit of national pride, also noticed a difference between the new settlers and the older residents; that the former were "far more industrious" than the latter. The majority of these new immigrants, of course, were settling in the Piedmont, which offered a healthier location than the eastern lowlands with disease-infested swamps and rivers; a factor that might explain their healthier appearance or more industrious attitude.[8]

James Iredell's tutor and brother-in-law, Samuel Johnston, wished that some of the industrious newcomers would journey to the East instead of the West. In a letter to a British relative he wrote that it was little wonder that people migrated to North Carolina "where the mere necessaries of life are so easily acquired, a country capable of feeding more than ten times the number of Inhabitants which at present inhabit it." But of all the immigrants who had come, not one had "landed within two hundred miles" of Edenton, where landowners also needed "honest industrious Farmers to Cultivate their Lands, instead of [the] Wretches" that they then employed.[9] Unfortunately for Johnston, the migrants moved west partly because of the

3

legendary tales about the richness of the western lands and partly because of the migratory patterns or routes established.

The Scotch-Irish, German, and English migrations from Pennsylvania and Maryland to the West (the Piedmont) began in the 1740s, but the influx of settlers did not become noticeable until the 1750s. By the end of 1750 eighty-two identifiable persons had located between the Yadkin and the Catawba rivers (Rowan County). Most of these individuals had come down the Great Wagon Road from Maryland and Pennsylvania. The road, an Indian trading path in earlier days, ran through western Maryland and the Shenandoah Valley right into the North Carolina Piedmont. It became the avenue by which large numbers of immigrants found their way to the fertile western lands. In the years 1754 to 1770, the inhabitants of Rowan County quadrupled, and the rate of increase was much faster by the latter year. In comparing Rowan's growth to an eastern county, Onslow's population did not quite double in those same years. In the northern, interior counties, such as Granville and Halifax, a number of Virginians were also coming across the border.[10]

Those individuals who came south left few specific accounts of their reasons for migrating, but the prospects of cheap land and high wages certainly appealed to them at a time when Pennsylvania, Maryland, and eastern Virginia were becoming crowded. These new settlers would doubtless have agreed with Colonel William Few's father who wanted a milder climate and a more fertile country than that offered by Maryland. The Few family was not disappointed in the father's choice of Orange County as their new residence.[11]

In contrast to the northern movement, the Scottish settlers migrated directly from Europe to Wilmington and then journeyed up the Cape Fear River to Anson and Cumberland counties. They tended to settle as family groups and in many cases the newly arrived individuals of the 1770s, such as William Gordon, settled near relatives. The colonial government encouraged this migration although the English authorities were beginning to fear its consequences — of removing worthy citizens from the British Isles. North Carolina officials had, on occasion, set aside lands for the Highlanders and had exempted them from the payment of taxes for a few years after their arrival.[12]

Because of the British government's concern at losing so many Highlanders, customs officials questioned a number of emigrants as they left port. These emigrants inevitably mentioned the high rents, low wages, the high cost of bread due to distilling grain into whiskey, the transference of farm land to sheep pastures and low cattle prices. On the other hand, Carolina offered them high wages and plenty of provisions and cheap land; in short, they went "for a better way of doing." The age of these emigrants averaged around twenty-five years, but it was kept low by the numbers of children who were leaving with their parents. The migration was very much a family affair as shown also by the sex ratio. About three males to every two females migrated. One customs report noted that tradesmen had little reason economically to leave Scotland, but that they were still going to America because of their families, which is not surprising because of the strong clannish ties of the Highlanders. A new country would obviously welcome such a stable group into its midst.[13]

North Carolina, then, early became a "melting pot," although the cosmo-politan nature of the population can be and has been over-emphasized. On the basis of the 1790 census, approximately 66 per cent of the inhabi-tants still had English surnames. The Scots, next to the English population in size, numbered only 14.8 per cent of the population. The Irish (both Ulster and Free State) made up 11.1 per cent of the population while only 4.7 per cent of the residents could be connected to a German background.[14] Persons of English ancestry were generally located in the coastal region, but they were also found in the West. The Scotch-Irish, primarily from Pennsylvania and Maryland, and the Germans, also from those colonies, settled mainly in the Piedmont. The Scots, generally from the Highlands, but sometimes from the Lowlands, especially merchants, were mainly found in the upper Cape Fear area. These latter three groups tended to settle together according to their ethnic and religious backgrounds. The Highland Scots and Germans spoke their own language, and, with the Scotch-Irish, they all maintained their own ministers and schoolmasters. They thus managed to maintain their separate identities even though they lived in an English colony. That they owed their first allegiance to their families or neighbors, however, had a decentralizing effect upon the colony as a whole.

Whether all the settlers had their expectations fulfilled is another ques-tion. Whether the image proved ephemeral or became reality depended largely on the settler and his attitude towards a frontier society — one where there was plenty of provisions but where the social order was constantly changing and manners were cast aside. John Macrae, a Scottish High-lander, captured both the image of the land and its reality in a Gaelic lullaby composed for his daughter. He promised her that in this new land, "We'll find suitors abounding in wealth and fame," as well as ample provisions — "nuts and apples and the sugar will grow" in the spring. Yet, in the face of this bounty, he found that, "Little do I like some of those who are here,/with their drugget coats and tall hats on their head,/and their scanty breeches split to the belt." To Macrae, the prospect of maintaining civilized manners in this wilderness seemed dim: "We're turned into Indians surely enough." To enjoy the fruits of the land and to prosper entailed not only hard labor, but also the ease with which one could accept frontier living conditions and primitive social institutions. Governor Martin worried that a number of the Highlanders would not survive, mainly because they were "unskilled in the Arts of Agriculture," (perhaps, because they were also ill-equipped for frontier living).[15]

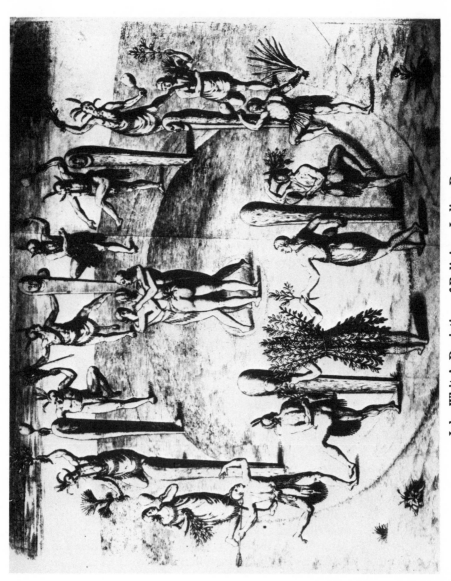

John White's Depiction of Religious Indian Dance

6

Not all North Carolina residents could anticipate an improvement in their socioeconomic status, even though for many individuals the colony symbolized opportunity and hope. The native Indian population in the East for instance was continually growing smaller until the remnants of the once powerful Tuscaroras (155 Indians) decided in 1767 to join their Iroquois relatives in New York. The Catawbas, who resided in Mecklenburg County, posed no threat to the white settlers and were primarily a novelty for local residents to show off to visitors. In 1761 they numbered only about 120 males "and a suitable number of Women"; the previous winter their population had been drastically reduced by a smallpox epidemic. The 1761 figure appears too small, however, since Elkanah Watson who visited the tribe in 1786 stated in that year that the tribe had been reduced to about a thousand people. Only the Cherokees to the west of settlement, with about 2,000 fighting men, had any sizable population and had yet to feel the full impact of the western movement of white farmers. The Indians hardly benefitted from the white migrant's image of North Carolina. Although their cultures were threatened, they at least managed to escape enslavement.[16]

The black population, involuntary immigrants, remained, for the most part, in a fixed status. They constituted an important element in the colony's demographic makeup. There were never as many slaves in North Carolina as in South Carolina where they made up 60 per cent of the population or in Virginia where they were at least 40 per cent of the inhabitants, but by 1760 in the Lower Cape Fear and Albemarle regions, the peculiar institution had become significant. Over 50 per cent of the households in both New Hanover and Chowan counties owned at least one slave. In contrast, less than 10 per cent of the households in Anson and Orange counties had any direct contact with slavery. By 1780 slaves numbered over 50 per cent of the population of New Hanover County and between 40 and 50 per cent in the northern and northeastern counties of Chowan, Gates, Halifax, and Granville. The western counties continued to have a much smaller proportion of blacks — generally less than 20 per cent of the population.[17]

Because exact population figures are difficult to ascertain for North Carolina before 1790, demographers usually figure on the basis of tax lists that there were three whites to every one black during the Revolutionary Era. The 1790 census indicates that the ratio for that year was three to one. The white-black ratio during the late colonial period, then, must have remained fairly constant. But just as the number of North Carolina's white inhabitants increased dramatically during the latter part of the colonial period, so also did the number of blacks; approximately 89 per cent, for example, in the years 1755 to 1767. The growth was not due to large shipments of slaves for sale since merchants generally dealt with only a few Negroes at a time. Few slaves immigrated with white families. The increase, then, represented primarily a natural increase and was located in those counties where the institution was already significant. Consequently a smaller percentage of the population was actually holding slaves by the time that the colony became a state, but individual holdings were larger.[18]

Slaveholding was concentrated in those counties where planters were producing for either the British or foreign markets: where the production of naval stores and tobacco was especially important, and rice cultivation was beginning to take place. The fact that Virginians and South Carolinians had early settled in those areas doubtless explained the presence of some slaves from the beginning of settlement. Outside of naval stores production or large scale tobacco or rice cultivation, most North Carolina farmers had little use for slave labor. Geography, then, because it helped to delay a large-scale commercial development of the colony, indirectly retarded the widespread growth of a slaveholding aristocracy.

Although North Carolina had plenty of rivers and sounds, they were shallow, and, with the exception of the Cape Fear River, they did not empty directly into the ocean. Instead there was a natural barrier of sand reefs and bars, which, with the treacherous waters that they partly produced, obstructed ocean-going traffic. In earlier days, pirates had found protection in the coastal area, but colonial and English merchants looked at the Capes, the shallow waters, bars and sand reefs in a far different light. Once in port shippers often had to dispatch smaller boats to go further up the rivers to collect cargo, which was a time-consuming task. The longest part of a voyage for a ship could well be the time that it spent in collecting goods along the North Carolina coast and rivers and in waiting for proper weather to set sail. One New England captain wrote to his employer that he had been "laying at Ocracock" for over two weeks as a result of a storm. During that time he had seen "fourteen sail of vessells drove on shore, and five ... entirely lost." In addition one was driven "over the South breakers and gone to see and every soul perished."[19]

Because of the inconvenience and often the expense of the eastern market, western or northern planters sent their surplus goods to Virginia or Charles Town. As a result, the colony did not always receive full credit for its exports. Sending goods overland also meant expense and time, so that a really profitable internal market system had yet to develop. Governor Arthur Dobbs noted that goods came "by Inland Carriage from Virginia and South Carolina," as well as "by Shipping to the several Ports" and the reverse was also true. His successor, Governor William Tryon, wanted to improve "communications between the western frontier counties and Brunswick port." He hoped to "bring Down" the commodities of the backcountry "which at present are diverted to South Carolina, a Circumstance as it adds to the Credit of Charlestown exports, lessens in the same proportion those of this province." The Moravians who ordinarily sent their goods to Charles Town experimented with the eastern market upon Tryon's encouragement. Unfortunately for the Wilmington and Brunswick merchants, the Moravians found that the commodities that they needed were scarce, that the prices were extremely high and that "they had to take goods in exchange for what they had brought" instead of money. After Cross Creek became a viable market center, the Moravians regularly sent goods there in exchange for commodities such as salt.[20]

The author of *American Husbandry* understood very well why North Carolina was still underdeveloped in the 1770s; why few people had settled in the colony even though the Piedmont was endowed with especially fertile fields. He noted the absence of a major trading town and good ports: he found "not one good one [port] in all North Carolina," while the major rivers all flowed into South Carolina. At the same time he concluded that these obstacles had advantageously pushed settlement westward, where the most fertile land was located. Settlement, indeed, had pushed westward, and, as a result, the majority of farmers were busily cultivating the soil primarily for their own sustenance, were making their own clothing and furniture, and, if they had a surplus, were taking it to the local merchant to buy salt, rum, or molasses. Even the larger farmers had not yet become specialists.[21]

Geography did not retard all large-scale commercial development. North Carolina's chief exports included various naval stores (tar, pitch, turpentine, and rosin) and lumber (boards, staves, and shingles). She ranked number one among the British continental colonies in the export of naval stores, producing seven-tenths of all tar; one-fifth of all pitch; and one-half of all turpentine — a total annual value of £42,000 sterling, which was three-fifths of the total value of naval stores exported from all the colonies. North Carolina "Tarheels" early discovered the wealth of their forests, and, as one traveller pointed out: "it is the forests which supply the present inhabitants of North Carolina not merely an occupation and a support, but the means as well of an easier life and often considerable estates." It sometimes took "considerable estates," however, to become involved in naval stores production — at least if one wanted to accumulate large profits rapidly. Large landholdings and large slaveholdings seemed to be prerequisites for the venture. Most naval stores came from the southeastern coastal area where both types of holdings prevailed, as well as where the longleaf pine, the necessary ingredient, grew profusely. Doubtless there were small farmers who also exploited the forests, but they could not compete on the same level as the large producer. Quantity counted.[22]

In the production of naval stores, making turpentine represented the simplest operation. A worker tapped the tree and then collected the sap from the so-called boxes (cuts in the bark) at regular intervals during the summer months. One slave could supposedly handle 3,000 boxes, which would make about 100 barrels of turpentine annually. If the turpentine were distilled into oil or spirits of turpentine, the residue became rosin, which could be used for varnish. The process of making tar and pitch required "a more considerable apparatus, and much greater trouble than turpentine," according to one traveller, with much justification. The producer first had to build a kiln-like structure, in which he piled up pieces of wood. Under the floor of the kiln he placed barrels "to receive the tarr" as it ran out once the firing had been started. Green tar, the preferred commodity, was made from freshly felled trees, probably those that had been used previously for turpentine. But, for the most part, dead trees were used in the process. To make pitch, one boiled the tar either "in an iron kettle" or in "a hole in the Ground." Under such crude conditions, it is little wonder that British merchants often complained about the quality of Carolina naval stores.[23]

While turpentine was summer business, tar was a winter affair. "By the use of wind-falls, dead trees, and those that have been boxed for turpentine, the people make money almost from nothing," according to one account, since in areas where tar was not made, "such wood rots in the forest."[24] Large landholders clearly were favored in the production of naval stores and found it far more profitable than planting their land. In addition, slaves could work all year around; indeed, a very efficient operation. But the small farmer, who owned new land and virgin timber, could also make a little money.

Wood products (sawn lumber, staves, shingles) represented North Carolina's third major export. One-seventh of all lumber from the continental colonies came from North Carolina and over 50 per cent of that lumber went to the West Indies. Between 55 per cent and 65 per cent of Carolina staves exported and between 50 and 60 per cent of shingles exported came from Ports Currituck and Roanoke in the Albemarle. The geography of that region was more conducive to the production of those articles than naval stores because of the presence of a variety of trees including cypress and oak, which grew well in the swampy bottom lands. The making of staves and shingles could also be small operations; neither process necessitated a large labor force.[25]

Sawn lumber, on the other hand, came mainly from Port Brunswick on the Cape Fear: 70 to 75 per cent of that exported. Because of the existence of many waterways there plus the presence of men who had available money to put into sawmilling operations, the Cape Fear and its tributaries were natural locations for the manufacture of sawn boards. By the 1760s sawmilling was clearly becoming important to that area. In 1764 there were about forty sawmills on the Cape Fear River. Two years later, Governor Tryon wrote that there were fifty mills "in repair and more building." All of these mills were located on the northeast and northwest branches of the Cape Fear and were apparently owned by men of some wealth. Janet Schaw, the often-quoted "Lady of Quality" from Scotland, found Councillor John Rutherfurd's sawmill "the finest I ever met with," and for her to make such an admission, the mill must indeed have been a fine one. She mentioned that it cut 3,000 boards a day and could "double the number when necessity demands it." The boards were then sent down river by rafts. The Rutherfurd operation was doubtless included in Tryon's number. Other ports, however, did send out some sawn lumber. In 1765 a traveller noted a sawmill on the Chowan River that was owned by Richard Brownrigg, a wealthy Edenton merchant.[26] The forests contributed greatly to North Carolina's economic well-being.

The number two export was provisions including corn, pork, beef, fish, wheat, peas, and beans. These articles mainly went to the West Indies, where the large sugar plantations depended on an outside food supply. Corn was the most valuable of the group, and North Carolina exported one-eleventh of all corn sent from the continental colonies. With respect to other provisions she supplied one-eighth of all pork and beef; three-tenths of one per cent of fish; less than one per cent of wheat; and 4 per cent of peas and beans. These products together made up only one-twenty-fifth of the total amount of provisions exported from the continental colonies, but they were still worth almost £20,000 sterling. Farmers doubtless cultivated several of the crops at one time and then exchanged them to local merchants for manufactured goods. Corn and tobacco or wheat and tobacco were often raised together on the same plantation as main money crops. Farmers could easily grow other articles, though, that might produce a surplus, which could be sold to the local storekeeper; for example, a field of peas and/or beans. In addition, with the many streams that ran through the countryside, the farmer could easily turn fisherman and supplement his income in that fashion. In fact, people upstream often complained to the General Assembly about sawmills cutting off their fish supply. In some cases, fishing became big business and could consume a person's whole energy as the people of Edenton discovered when their local rector became a "herring catching parson."[27]

North Carolina farmers did not enjoy the best reputations in the various accounts left by travellers. Only the Moravians lived up to European or northern standards and impressed various visitors with their fine farms and good crops. Janet Schaw found that American farmers did not trouble "themselves with improvements." Even her brother to her embarrassment had lost all memory of how to farm properly: "every instrument of husbandry was unknown here; not only all the various ploughs, but all the machinery used with such success at home, and that the only instrument used is a hoe, with which they at once till and plant the corn." Nor did they use fertilizer. Her sister-in-law "was shocked at the mention of our manuring the ground, and declared she never would eat corn that grew thro' dirt." (Miss Schaw did not mention that Scottish farmers themselves were only beginning to use the latest agricultural techniques.)[28]

The Scottish lady also criticized the manner by which Carolina farmers cared for their livestock — "the cattle must provide for themselves or starve." She was not alone in such sentiments. Cattle, hogs, sheep — all livestock — roamed loose and fended for themselves; especially the hogs who primarily lived on acorns and pine seeds. Only before they were marketed did they receive a little corn. More care was provided the cattle. As one traveller pointed out: "by penning up the calves, and throwing out a little corn every day to the dams, the milch cows have been accustomed to come up to the dwelling-house from time to time to be milked." But in the winter cattle also lived off the land, primarily on moss.[29]

The size of North Carolina cattle herds, especially in the West, has been exaggerated partly because of contemporary testimony and partly because of the traditional beliefs that large herds of cattle always roam a frontier; at least an American frontier. The writer of *American Husbandry* mentioned "the vast herds of cattle kept by the planters." He believed that it was not at all uncommon "to see one man the master of from 300 to 1,200, and even to 2,000 cows, bulls, oxen and young cattle; hogs also in prodigious numbers." But actually there were larger livestock holdings in the East than in the West. One study has concluded that the average number of cattle per owner, about 1780, ranged from a high of sixteen cattle per owner for the eastern county of Chowan to six for the western county of Wilkes. Few herds exceeded 100 and none could be found that exceeded 300. Not all counties, however, were included in the survey.[30]

One county omitted because of lack of tax data was Edgecombe. In a recent analysis of Edgecombe inventories, cattle owners averaged thirty-one head and there were eight herds that exceeded 100; two of which exceeded 300. One man owned 396 head and another individual possessed 412. The author of this study believed that earlier revisionist figures have been too small. But Edgecombe still fits the pattern established by the previous writers: it was a wealthy county in comparison to many of the others and was in the East. It still had available lands but was in a settled area, which would make cattle raising profitable; nor were the size of its herds that far out of line with herds in Cumberland County. The Edgecombe example might very well indicate a higher average than sixteen per owner, but not nearly as high as contemporaries estimated.[31]

While the large herds impressed travellers, they all believed that northern beef and pork were better. Governor Josiah Martin, however, blamed the taste of North Carolina pork on the salt used instead of how the hogs were raised. Shortly after he arrived in the colony he reported that salted pork was "made in vast quantities," but that it did not keep as well as northern pork because of inferior salt. Martin wanted repealed the parliamentary statute that prevented the direct importation of Portuguese salt to Carolina ports. He correctly called pork a leading export, but North Carolina did not receive credit for all her livestock sales since many were taken overland to Pennsylvania and Virginia markets.[32]

Not only North Carolina livestock was sold in Virginia, but much tobacco was also shipped overland. Tobacco, often thought of as a leading export only ranked fourth on North Carolina's export list and could hardly compare with the quantity exported by Virginia and Maryland. Approximately 50 per cent of North Carolina's tobacco crop, however, went through Virginia ports, so that the exact amount produced is difficult to ascertain. The counties north of Albemarle Sound were especially associated with the growing of tobacco, and in those counties slavery was an important factor. The holdings were not as large as in the Cape Fear but between 40 and 60 per cent of the households owned a few slaves. Along the northern border in Northampton, Halifax, and Granville, where many Virginians had settled, tobacco cultivation was common. And by the time the War for Independence broke out, tobacco exports were not only increasing, but its cultivation was spreading southward.[33]

An example of the spread is found in the economy of Edgecombe County. By the 1750s three inspection warehouses had been established in the county. In the mid-sixties tobacco production dropped, but in 1770 it began to increase once more. Evidently the percentage of people involved in commercial production, however, was small; less than 20 per cent of the total population. In keeping with the need for slaves in a tobacco-raising region, over 50 per cent of Edgecombe households owned slaves. By 1775, 13 per cent of those households possessed eleven or more slaves, which places the county in the same category as New Hanover. The author of *American Husbandry* did not think that North Carolina's climate was any better for tobacco than Virginia's, but he saw a greater production in the future for North Carolina because of the newness of the soil. The Edgecombe example would substantiate his view.[34]

Writers have often considered rice and indigo production as characterizing the Lower Cape Fear region. While it is true that that is where those crops were cultivated and that they played a significant role, naval stores were by far the number one export of the area. Rice and indigo required large amounts of labor as well as large landholdings to be profitable. Only in the Lower Cape Fear was the labor situation as well as the climate favorable to production of those crops, but even there men of capital devoted little acreage to them. What was cultivated was on an experimental basis. Governor Martin, writing in 1772, noted that several planters on the Cape Fear were experimenting with rice and indigo in "the South Carolina manner." In 1771 when the largest amount of rice was exported in the years 1768 to 1775, no more than 500 acres could possibly have been planted, according to one estimate. Newspaper advertisements in mentioning land for sale that would be good for rice cultivation stopped short of saying whether the land had actually been used for that purpose. If the land had been cultivated in rice, the acreage cleared was small — usually about thirty acres.[35]

All of the major crops were subject to a system of inspection to maintain the quality of the colony's exports. Beginning early in the eighteenth century, inspection laws had been passed but were apparently not enforced well because of innumerable complaints about North Carolina products. Governor Tryon, writing in 1767, found that it was with some justification that "the Product of this Colony" had been "thought of a worse quality when exported than that of its neighbors." He believed that the situation was due to "the slovenly way of coppering, dressing, pickling and filling the commodity for exportation and to the fraud and deceit of those who make the goods." Tryon referred to an act passed in 1764 that set the regulations that were primarily followed during the Revolutionary Era. By that act, the county court appointed the local inspectors, and Tryon mentioned that as the local justices of the peace were often "the largest exporters of the Co[unty] — The Inspector is often frustrated then — especially if he wants to keep his job." The inspection system continued — but so also did the complaints.[36]

The government also intervened in the economy by giving bounties for the raising of hemp and flax. Note has already been made of at least the verbal encouragement given to rice and indigo growers. Indigo, of course, received a bounty from the British government under the navigation system. Tryon and Dobbs were continually encouraging a diversified economy including some manufacturing. Tryon was especially interested in improving communication between East and West, so that the backcountry trade would come to a North Carolina port instead of South Carolina or Virginia. He also wanted to see a distinction made in the naval office records between North Carolina and South Carolina exports and the establishment of a mail service.[37]

Despite geographic obstacles and a sparse population, then, North Carolina exports were worth over £80,000 sterling and if minor commodities such as skins were added, the total value of exports from North Carolina ports reached at least £100,000 sterling. In comparison to her neighbors, North Carolina's trade was small. Virginia's exports equalled £562,000 sterling and South Carolina's totalled £429,000 sterling. But some of the Virginia and South Carolina exports had originally come from North Carolina. If the colony had received full credit for all her goods, her exports might well have doubled. Officially, the volume of exports sent from North Carolina ports exceeded only two other colonies, New Hampshire and New Jersey; nevertheless North Carolina's economy was flourishing by the late colonial period.[38] She was primarily an agricultural society, but she had gone beyond the stage of bare subsistence. While her farmers were not specialists, they produced enough crops so that they could engage in some trade and buy a few manufactured products.

Imports into the colony, approximately the same total value as exports, consisted mainly of British manufactured goods, salt, refined sugar, spices, beverages, rum, and molasses. They came either from the northern colonies or from Britain directly. Small shipments of slaves were occasionally brought in from the West Indies, but the slave trade was relatively unimportant compared to the South Carolina market. For example, in the year ending April, 1775, only 125 slaves were brought into Port Brunswick — the major port for the Cape Fear area where the greatest demand for slave labor existed. In comparison, over 8,000 slaves were brought into Charles Town in 1773. Ordinarily merchants or ship captains brought in just a few slaves. In that trade as well as in expensive manufactured articles, North Carolina merchants were rather cautious about large consignments.[39]

In the five years before the War for Independence, North Carolina sent the major part of her exports to the other continental colonies; nearly one-third of her products to the British Isles; about one-fourth to the West Indies and less than 5 per cent to southern European and African ports. While many North Carolina merchants owned their ships and carried on a considerable commerce, New England and British merchants, who maintained factors in the colony, played an important role in the economy. Ships often came from a northern port, stopped in North Carolina, then went on to the West Indies or Britain. On the other hand a direct trade between Britain and Carolina was increasing. Ships coming into port faced the difficulty of bringing in suitable cargo, and often times carried some ballast.[40] Although a flourishing trade was beginning to develop, the backcountry farmers were relatively unaffected by the trans-Atlantic or Caribbean aspects of North Carolina's trade. They were concerned with only the local merchant.

North Carolina merchants became deeply indebted to British mercantile houses, but that indebtedness did not reflect an unfavorable trade balance as much as it demonstrated the high insurance and shipping rates. As an example of the various charges encountered in a shipment, Robert Williams, New Bern merchant, sent a cargo in 1770 that included 798 barrels of tar, 35 barrels of pitch, and 444 barrels of turpentine. It also included ten barrels and five tierces of tallow, two barrels and three tierces of Beeswax, and one barrel of snake root. The sales plus the bounty given for naval stores totalled £1055.14.10 sterling, but in June, when the account was closed, Robert Williams received only £344 sterling for his share. In February, the customs duties had amounted to £132.15 while wharfage and officer's fees, freight and storage charges plus extra cooperage amounted to £497.45.04. In April and May, there were extra freight and wharfage charges which equalled £44.—.10. Commission and brokerage fees — each 2½ per cent of the total value — came to £26.12.22. Over two-thirds of the value of the product thus stayed in England and could not be applied to the purchase of manufactured articles to be brought to the colony.[41]

Richard Ellis, another New Bern merchant, fared better. Ellis sent a cargo of staves and headings on board one of his ships to his London correspondent, which sold for £507.6.6. Charges amounted to £10.1.5 and the commission was £12.13.6. One-half of the net proceeds, £192.5.9½, was paid to a

Captain Barnes, evidently the captain of the ship; the other half was credited to Ellis's account. On that particular voyage, Ellis made a 38 per cent profit. Other merchants besides Richard Ellis owned their ships, which helped a bit in reducing freight charges. The firm of Blount, Hewes and Blair in Edenton owned at one time ten vessels either fully or partially. Some of these ships were probably built in the colony, since Hewes operated a ship-yard.[42]

One northern merchant, Aaron Lopez of Newport, Rhode Island, took an active part in the Carolina trade, and the activities of his ship captains demonstrated some of the problems of the trade. A Lopez ship would bring various beverages including rum, molasses, and salt to Edenton or New Bern. There it would pick up naval stores, provisions and staves — various cooperage materials for the wine trade. These goods the ship then carried to the West Indies or Europe, picked up wine, molasses, manufactured goods and headed back to Newport. But voyages were sometimes delayed because of the Carolina connection. There the ships might encounter storms or problems with shallow water, a non-receptive market to certain manu-factured goods, competition from British or other northern merchants which meant low prices for manufactured goods but high prices for the raw materials, and poor warehouse facilities so that unpurchased goods caused a problem. And, then, there was always the problem of available money.[43]

Lopez's captains as well as his Carolina correspondents, Richard Ellis at New Bern and Cullen Pollock, a wealthy planter and trustworthy friend in Edenton, often wrote him about these difficulties. In January, 1772, Pollock wrote to Lopez that Captain English had "gone up Cushy to load with corn and staves as soon as the corn is fit to take on board for so long a Voyage, which will not be untill the last of February." He apologized to Lopez about the latter's misinformation concerning the Carolina market since "there never were shorter Crops made." Pollock had never seen so many vessels as were now in port. They all wanted corn, "and most of them have brought cash more or less." One could purchase staves, however, for goods. Three months later a Lopez captain, Peleg Greene, wrote about the shortage of staves in New Bern and Mr. Ellis's attempts to find some. "I have tryd the whole Town through and cannot purches any Heading or Staves, for here is three Vessell now loading for Jamaica who had engaged all in the place." On another occasion, Ellis had a hard time finding a place to store the salt brought in because it had been promised "the Country men" who had not yet come, so they were "ableag'd to make a store of the sloop."[44]

The local merchant, whether he lived in a seaport or in the country, became both wholesaler and retailer. "What are called shops in England, are known here by the appellation of stores, and supply the inhabitants with every individual article necessary in life," wrote one English visitor. The merchants sold "linens, woollens, silks, paper, books, iron, cuttery, hats, stockings, shoes, wines, spirits, sugars, &c. and even jewelry; for which in return they receive tobacco, skins, furs, cotton, butter, flour, &c. in considerable quantities at a time, being obliged to give a year's credit." The storeowner accepted produce with little hesitation, not only because of the lack of a circulating medium but also because of the value of the product. In competition with other New Bern merchants, Richard Ellis advertised that he gave "the highest prices for produce," and Ellis and other merchants easily extended credit. Although the lack of towns and currency hindered trade, they clearly did not halt it. The country store, situated at a crossroads, rivalled its town neighbor in prosperity. Granville County had no towns in the late colonial period, but it had forty-six firms that transacted business at some time during those years, and none went bankrupt, although they were often in court to collect debts.[45]

The firm of Johnston and Bennehan located at Snow Camp in Orange County carried on a flourishing business in the 1770s. When the firm first opened up direct connections with a British firm, the Alstons of Glascow, William Johnston and Richard Bennehan reminded the Scottish merchants that they were trying out some of the goods on a trial basis. Upon receipt of the first cargo, they mentioned that the goods arrived safely and were satisfactory except that some of the articles "were rather too high for this part of the Country." The articles imported generally included dry goods, clothes, books, tableware, tools and china, sugar, salt, and rum. The Snow Camp store's inventory was £532.16.4 North Carolina currency in March, 1770, but it increased over the years until in March, 1775, it was £1566.15.8 North Carolina currency. According to the store's accounts, the inventory was one-third the net worth of the store. In five years, then, the store's value had increased three times. During the war years, the inventory decreased, but the store began to prosper once more with the resumption of peace.[46]

In 1784 Johnston and Bennehan wrote to a London firm about opening up a trade for manufactured goods. They mentioned that previously (before the war), because of their limited trade and the "considerable distance from Navigation, we have in general found it more Convenient to sell produce here for Cash or Bills of Exchange than to Ship." They sometimes had managed in the past, however, to get together a tobacco cargo. Disposal of produce could be a problem for a small concern, but before the war Scottish factors resided in northern neighborhoods especially to purchase tobacco. In the case of Johnston and Bennehan, they generally sent their produce to Petersburg, Virginia, and obtained bills of exchange in return by which they could buy manufactured goods. The firm not only had to deal in produce, then, but also North Carolina currency and Virginia currency, in addition to the bills of exchange.[47]

There were large stores or outlets in the Piedmont, however, that dealt directly with the British mercantile houses and exchanged North Carolina products for manufactured goods. In most cases, these firms were branches of either a coastal company such as Hogg and Campbell (Wilmington) or a Scottish company such as John Hamilton and Company. Hogg and Campbell started out in Wilmington but early learned the value of having stores in the backcountry. They thus established themselves in Cross Creek and Hillsborough. Their annual profits amounted to £1,200 — a very comfortable sum for the period. John Hamilton and Company, one of the largest concerns in the colonies with operations in both Virginia and Carolina, estimated their profits between £4,000 and £5,000 sterling on the eve of the Revolution.[48] Large profits were partly due to large markups. John Hamilton and Company sold at approximately a 50 per cent wholesale markup and at retail a 100 per cent markup — which was not unusual. The Snow Camp store, for instance, had as much as 400 per cent markup on tools. In 1773 Wilmington merchant John Burgwin advertised his prices for goods "at advance of two & half for one from sterling invoice"; that is, he would sell goods at wholesale at two and one-half times their value in Great Britain. Out of those profits, of course, came the operation of the store and transportation rates, but prices were still extremely high in North Carolina.[49]

Farmers invariably became debtors to local merchants; North Carolina merchants to British creditors. Manufactured articles simply cost more than the raw materials exchanged for them. In a case in Perquimans County, farmer and cooper, William Foster, began trading with a local merchant, Malacky Jones, in June, 1769. He first "purchased a pair of brown thread stockings for eight shillings and a horse comb for eight pence." By December his purchases amounted to £4.7.2¼. In that month his account was credited with eighty-six pounds of pork, worth fifteen shillings, five pence, which reduced his debt to the store to 3.11.9½. In 1770 his debt increased to £5.19.11, even though he had brought in "22 bushels of wheat, 630 pieces of barrel heading, and 55 pounds of pork," which totaled £7.2. In 1771 his debt amounted to 8.8.9½. By May, 1773, Foster refused further payment; Jones refused further credit and brought suit against Foster. As to whether the case was resolved, the records remain silent.[50]

The Foster-Jones case was not exceptional. The accounts of various stores showed the enormous debts owed to merchants, and court records indicated the number of suits initiated to collect debts. As a result storeowners often became large landowners and speculators. Samuel Johnston, not considering the debtor's loss of property but sympathizing with eastern lawyers and merchants, complained that "debtors go off daly to the settlements to the Westward with all their objects." Their creditors had no "power to obtain any kind of indemnity for their Debts."[51] The West symbolized Frederick Jackson Turner's safety valve for various reasons.

Collecting debts was just one problem. Together with a lack of currency and inflation, it caused innumerable anxieties for people on various economic levels. On a visit to the Cape Fear from Edenton Samuel Johnston found "the usual scarcity of money." A friend, merchant Richard Quince, who had "thousands due to him" could at that time "command no money but by drawing Bills." Johnston had loaned him £12.[52] Quince at least had alternatives. Persons less wealthy without financial connections could find themselves in dire straits and the West offered the only solution.

The Reverend Mr. James Reed wrote in 1765 that "all sorts of wares and merchandize are excessive dear much dearer I believe in this province, than in any other on this continent which may in some measure be owing to our bad navigation but principally to the want of a proper staple commodity." In trying to find a place for the New Bern schoolmaster to live, although without much success, Reed found that board was "likewise very high." He also put in a word for the clergy; that under prevailing economic conditions, the legal stipend set by the Vestry Act could not satisfactorily support them. Two years later, another minister, Alexander Stewart, recalled that when he first came to the colony in 1754 "goods were then reasonable and provisions 100 per cent cheaper than at this day." Money was not only scarce, but contrary to the axiom that good money goes into hiding, it had not only disappeared but it had also depreciated! "So great is the distress of the people for want of a currency, that Mobs and Riots are frequent." Mr. Stewart blamed the "high advance upon Goods, the insufficiency of the exports, and the badness of our staple and navigation." These complaints came from the maritime districts of the province. But the regulators also noted as one of their grievances the want of a currency, which they especially felt when it came time to pay taxes. At least the people of the East had warehouse receipts for their tobacco and indigo by which they could pay taxes. The people on the frontier, because of the distance to the commercial areas, no doubt possessed less money, but whether they suffered from it more than the Cape Fear area raises a question since merchants there, largely independent of British connections, required currency for carrying on the trans-Atlantic or Caribbean trade. Only the northeastern counties seemed not to have suffered because of the presence of Virginia currency.[53]

How well off, then, was the average North Carolinian in the Revolutionary Era? He had little money, was indebted, lived in a small frame house or log cabin, was often deemed slovenly and lazy by contemporary visitors, and had little contact with the outside world. A later chapter will deal with how he lived, but economically he belonged to a large group of middling folk, many of whom believed that they lived comfortably; that they had the necessities of life even though they did not live luxuriously. He raised much of what he needed, but his diversified agriculture allowed him enough surplus to buy a few extras; perhaps some sugar or a new hat for his wife. The wealthiest 10 per cent of the population owned only between 35 and 40 per cent of the land; not quite as much as in the northern colonies where they owned about 45 per cent of the land and much less than in Virginia and South Carolina where the wealthiest 10 per cent owned between 50 and 60 per cent of the land. The landless laboring class (including slaves) constituted about a third of the population. On the frontier it comprised only about 20 per cent of the population. In contrast, in Virginia and South Carolina, the landless laboring class, including slaves, made up over half of the population. Especially in North Carolina lived many farmers on the frontier who had not bothered to take out land titles. Many laborers who had just arrived in the colony expected to work for wages only until they acquired enough savings to buy some land. As a result, the statement — that a third of the population was landless — may not give a truly accurate picture of the middling nature of North Carolina's society. Nevertheless, there was a more equitable distribution of wealth in North Carolina than in the neighboring colonies of South Carolina and Virginia, and its distribution of wealth compared favorably with the northern colonies, where there were fewer landless laborers (probably because there were fewer slaves); but the wealthiest in the North owned more land than North Carolina's wealthiest.[54]

Small farmers, not large planters, then, dominated the North Carolina landscape. Land grants were kept small — mostly between 100 and 300 acres — rarely exceeding 640 acres, at one time the legal limit for individual grants. The English-North Carolina speculator Henry McCulloh had managed to obtain about 1,200,000 acres in the 1730s and 1740s, but he was an exception. And in subdividing his land, McCulloh and his son surveyed it into tracts that were generally under 300 acres, which serves as a clue to the average-size holding. The McCullohs were particularly considering poor immigrants (including Highlanders) who could only afford small pieces of land. In a list of grants made between 1744 and 1755 in various counties, most landgrants fell into the range of 200 to 300 acres. In a study of Granville County, grants there primarily averaged between 340 and 450 acres. Because individual grants were kept small, of course, does not necessarily mean that holdings remained correspondingly small. Land was cheap and plentiful, which enabled a settler once established to dabble a bit in speculative ventures. Even an English visitor on the eve of the War for Independence could not help but purchase one 450 acre plantation, which was situated partly in Virginia and partly in North Carolina. At its sale he not only made a good profit but also noted the higher value of Virginia land. As the small land speculator was buying, however, he was doubtless selling some of his less desirable acreage. In addition, since land purchases were generally small, his holdings could hardly have become excessive.[55]

One study has indicated that the majority of North Carolina landowners in 1780 held less than 400 acres. Only in New Hanover County did 50 per cent of the land holdings exceed 400 acres; nearly 25 per cent of the New Hanover holdings exceeded 1,000 acres. The average size of holdings for the counties where statistics were available ranged from 933.7 acres in New Hanover County to 166.3 acres in Pasquotank. The mean fell at 420 acres. Professor Jackson Turner Main has estimated that in the backcountry "one-

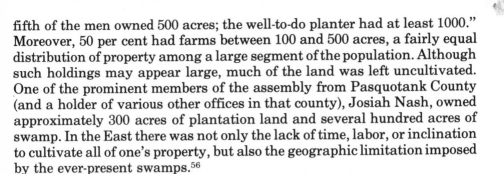

fifth of the men owned 500 acres; the well-to-do planter had at least 1000." Moreover, 50 per cent had farms between 100 and 500 acres, a fairly equal distribution of property among a large segment of the population. Although such holdings may appear large, much of the land was left uncultivated. One of the prominent members of the assembly from Pasquotank County (and a holder of various other offices in that county), Josiah Nash, owned approximately 300 acres of plantation land and several hundred acres of swamp. In the East there was not only the lack of time, labor, or inclination to cultivate all of one's property, but also the geographic limitation imposed by the ever-present swamps.[56]

By the Revolutionary Era, the gauge of wealth or economic status centered around land and slaves in the southern colonies. Most farmers had enough land to provide an income of £100 per annum by which they could live comfortably, but they had few if any slaves. Main concluded that a southern planter, to be considered wealthy, needed twenty slaves. Governor Tryon, shortly after arriving in North Carolina, described "A Plantation with Seventy Slaves on it ... a good property" and observed that "in the Counties on the Sea Coast Planters have from fifty to 250 Slaves.... When a man marries his Daughters he never talks of the fortune in money but 20 30 or 40 Slaves." From time to time he might also deliver "a Certain Number of Tarr or Turpentine Barrels, which serve towards exonerating the charges of the Wedding." If Tryon's statement is taken at face value, it would appear that many wealthy planters lived in North Carolina. But in 1769 (after this remark was made) only 6.7 per cent of the New Hanover households (the county with the heaviest slave concentration) held twenty-one slaves or more. Only eight households in the Lower Cape Fear in the late 1760s had more than fifty slaves. In the same context, there were only about ten to twenty large estates (2,000 to 5,000 acres) on the Lower Cape Fear on the eve of the Revolution.[57]

In Chowan County in the Albemarle region in 1777, eight men (one per cent of the taxables) owned property assessed at more than £7,800 North Carolina currency (or £5,000 sterling) and could thus be defined as being "truly wealthy"; another 6 per cent could be described as well-to-do with an assessed income over £3,125 (or £2,000 sterling); 68 per cent fell into the moderate range, and 25 per cent either owned property assessed below £100 or held no property at all. Interestingly enough, the wealthiest members of the county did not own an excessive amount of land. Only four men owned more than 1,000 acres in Chowan, although some individuals probably owned land in other counties, which the tax lists did not reflect. The number of slaves owned by the wealthy ranged from twenty to 125.[58]

The estate of Samuel Johnston, one of the wealthiest residents of Chowan County, was valued at over £10,000 North Carolina currency. The Chowan tax list noted that Johnston owned 635 acres and forty-two slaves, but Johnston owned land in Pasquotank, and his own tax memorandum indicated that he possessed nearly 2,000 acres of land and fifty-two slaves in 1777. Johnston belonged to the wealthiest segment of the community, and individuals looked to him for both social and political leadership. The favored nephew of a former governor, Gabriel Johnston, he owned one of the most handsome homes and the largest library in the colony. But his holdings scarcely compared in magnitude with many of his Virginia peers who owned thousands of acres of land and at least one hundred slaves. A decade earlier Johnston, then in his early thirties, wrote to his uncle in Scotland that he and his brother were "in tolerable Business and this not in the way of being very rich, yet we have a prospect of making competent fortunes." How "competent" Johnston believed his fortune was in 1777 one can only guess, but by then he had clearly become one of the wealthiest members of the community.[59]

In a study of the economic status of the North Carolina Council, supposedly the men of the "Better Sort," acreages held by members in the Revolutionary Era ranged from 512 acres to 800,000 (the latter belonging to speculator Henry Eustace McCulloh). Most of the councillors fell into the range of 1,000 to 4,000 acres. With respect to slaves, some apparently owned none while only William Dry held more than 100. The figures appear incomplete but the council members, in relationship to the South Carolina Council with whom they were compared, were not nearly as wealthy, though they might have been on a "similar economic plane."[60]

All of this information is not to say that there were not men of extreme wealth. There were. John Rutherfurd valued his estate at over £21,000 sterling. It contained more than 4,000 acres of land, although only 300 acres were cleared and planted with corn and other grains, and 150 slaves, including many valuable tradesmen. Also on the estate was a sawmill, a smith's forge, much virgin timber, 150 head of livestock, and twenty oxen. The land produced several thousand barrels of pitch, tar, turpentine, and shingles. In earlier years Rutherfurd had gone bankrupt but had managed to become wealthy once more by the time the War for Independence broke out. Rutherfurd owed much of that new wealth to his marriage with Governor Gabriel Johnston's widow — which brought him into a controversial relationship with the Johnston clan. Not all North Carolinians were so fortunate in their alliances, but many persons still found the colony very much a land of opportunity. Samuel Johnston wrote that here was a bountiful future for any "one who is not disabled by infirmities." And though they might come from rather humble origins, they could hope with good reason to become men of substance.[61]

How comfortably people lived depended not only on their economic circumstances, but also on their own view of society and their economic and social expectations. The idea of owning land and being able to secure a living from it must have satisfied the expectations of many individuals. But whether they made the most of what they had and whether they had achieved a high standard of living can also be evaluated from the view of other observers. In a paradoxical description of Piedmont living standards, an English gentleman travelling in North Carolina on the eve of the Revolution found "a great many very fine farms, and a number of excellent mills" near Hillsborough. On the other hand the inhabitants of the area, primarily Scotch-Irish and German, were "the very lowest and most ignorant class, who export large quantities of exceeding good butter and flour, in waggons ... besides multitudes of fat cattle, beeves, and hogs." He found that "almost every man in this country has been the fabricator of his own fortune, and many of them are very opulent," despite the fact that he found the majority of them wretched, ignorant, and slovenly.[62]

What the English visitor saw was a highly mobile society; both a horizontal and a vertical mobility. Adventurous farmers were continually moving westward; once poor immigrants were acquiring land; especially ambitious yeomen were moving up the socioeconomic ladder by the acquisition of more land, which generally meant an improved social status in the community, but not always the acquisition of the social amenities. Not all individuals, of course, were touched by the economic prosperity or opportunity that many North Carolinians were enjoying. Although blacks contributed by their labor a great deal to the economy and the economic well-being of their masters, they did not share in the fruits of that labor. In the push westward by the sturdy white yeomen, Indians could only lose land. And North Carolina did not escape (as most communities do not) the presence of the dependent poor who remain in that condition.

North Carolina, however, was basically a rural middle-class (middling) society. There was a much more equitable distribution of property than in the other southern colonies. She had both wealthy and poor residents, but the wealthy were not as wealthy as in other colonies and the poor represented a smaller percentage of the general population than in the other southern colonies. Most individuals fell between the extremes; at least two-thirds of the population owned some property. Some of the landless residents no doubt "squatted" on land; the rapid flow of new settlers meant a source of laborers who eventually intended to purchase land. A majority of the population, then, fell into that group best described as yeoman freeholders who worked their land with the help of their families. As far as they were concerned they were engaged in good, hard, honest labor, which brought them real wealth. Some of that group did not intend to stay in their yeoman status but realized that with labor and frugality, they could acquire a "competent" fortune.

As small property-holders they also had a voice in their government, although they were not all that tied to it. Because of the sparse population and distances from one farm to another or one town to another, their closest ties were with their families and neighbors, and, in the case of ethnic groups, their churches. Especially the farmers in the interior had little contact with any representative of the Establishment — whether it be royal officials, Anglican clergymen, or eastern merchants. Many of their own county officials had come from the middling rank. It is little wonder, then, that North Carolina society sparked a disgusting aura of equality as far as some of the more genteel observers were concerned.

CHAPTER II

THE SOCIAL ORDER AND A CLASH OF VALUES

Contemporary observers of colonial society generally placed British-Americans in three social classes: the "Better Sort," the "Middling," and the "Lower Sort." By far, the large majority of colonials fell in-between and enjoyed a comfortable living; that is, they possessed the necessities of life and could also afford a few luxuries. Even the "Better Sort," for reasons of political expediency, sometimes identified themselves with the "middling folk," while the "lower sort" had much opportunity for upward mobility. In short, the values of colonial society were primarily middle-class values, but given its basically middle-class nature, colonial society still had a definite class structure and individuals were conscious of their position within that structure. Writers commonly point to the southern colonies as being especially aristocratic — doubtless because of the presence of the plantation system based on large land holdings and slave labor. But it can be argued, with a good deal of evidence, that colonial society itself, as it was maturing, had become more stratified (or more aristocratic) by the time of the Revolution. In the past, historians have held that feudalism could not have been established in the New World because of the vast amount of land and the freedom from restrictive European institutions. But it is just as plausible to argue that the primitive conditions of the seventeenth century New World prevented the growth of feudal institutions; that in the eighteenth century there was a feudalistic revival; and that the Revolution halted this aristocratic tendency.[1]

In the colonial society of the 1760s and the 1770s the "Better Sort" monopolized economic, social, and political leadership. What placed a man in this category? — not only wealth (which certainly counted) but *prestige*. He had to be a gentleman — to behave with moderation, virtue, and honor — a man who cultivated the arts as well as his "mental powers." If not formally educated, he at least had to be well-read and needed to possess a multi-volumed library. With self-assurance he assumed a personal responsibility for managing public affairs in the best interests of the community. He knew his role in society and acted accordingly; he married within his station and raised his children who subsequently learned their place in the social order. His position could be challenged by an "upstart," but by the Revolutionary Era, in most colonies, certain families had come to dominate colonial affairs. Inheritance of position, however, counted little if it were not accompanied by property. Large planters in the South and wealthy merchants in the North formed the basis of the upper class, but professional men were often included as well. To exert effective leadership an individual needed both respect and money.

In North Carolina, as has already been pointed out, lived men of the "Better Sort." But in the case of many families their credentials were not firmly established and they were still struggling for social acceptance. After all, North Carolina had long been a frontier province, and only after mid-eighteenth century was it beginning to prosper and gain a sizable population. Most North Carolina residents doubtless identified themselves with one of the social classes, but because there was a wider distribution of property in the colony than in the other southern colonies, the "Better Sort" did not stand out as clearly on the socioeconomic ladder. Nor, as pointed out earlier, were they as prosperous as their Virginia or South Carolina peers. Only certain eastern families had the aristocratic background that qualified them for leadership in the traditional British-American meaning. Many individuals who might strive for social and political leadership were recent arrivals and were not identified as being firmly attached to the welfare of the colony.

Most North Carolina gentlemen were planters, but a few were merchants and lawyers and, to a lesser degree, doctors and clergymen. Many combined several occupations; for example, large planters who were engaged in the production of naval stores or tobacco for overseas markets often became merchants. On the other hand, many merchants, including the many representatives of Scottish firms who had moved to North Carolina in the late colonial period, purchased plantations, which not only provided them with a sound investment, but also gave them added status in the community. Merchants oftentimes ended up with extensive land holdings because of mortgage foreclosures and, as a result, became land speculators on the side. Some of them gained enough influence in their local communities to be elected to the General Assembly, and many of them married daughters of the leading planters. Janet Schaw noted that "all the merchants of any note" in Wilmington were British "and many of them very genteel people." She also added that "they all disapprove of the present proceedings," (revolutionary activities) — an overstatement on Miss Schaw's part.[2]

A number of lawyers also found opportunity in North Carolina because of the colony's rapid economic development and growing population — especially on the frontier where there was a demand for various legal services, including the registration of land titles and the settlement of suits surrounding disputed landholdings. Various government jobs, such as clerkships in the courts, also beckoned would-be lawyers. The demand for attorneys brought a variety of men — including some rather disreputable individuals. When James Iredell's uncle, a merchant in the West Indies, heard that his nephew was reading law, he wished him success but warned him that the profession was "dangerous to virtue in all countries, but more especially in your Colony, where persons can with so much ease, qualify themselves for its practice." He believed that there were many of these "petty-foggers" who reside in North Carolina. Cullen Pollock, an Edenton resident, in writing about a recently deceased friend, commented that "he was a Gentleman of the Law possessed of every Virtue, and of a Liberal Education, he was the only one of that Profession, that ever I knew, whose acquaintance with the most vilinous part of Mankind had not deprived [him] of the feelings of humanity."[3] The fact that lawyers were often admired for their knowledge and manners explains why many managed to obtain upper class status. Their legal training enabled them to assume political leadership easily, and, as a result, planters often had their sons educated in the law.

Some doctors also managed to attain upper class status. Waightstill Avery recorded in his diary that he spent one night with Dr. William Cathcart, "a gentleman of extraordinary fine sense and great reading." Avery also admired the doctor's daughters, "possessed of the three greatest motives to be courted: Beauty, Wit and Prudence, and Money." Samuel Johnston felt the same way about Dr. Cathcart and further cemented his friendship by entering "into a connection of a very tender Nature" with the eldest daughter. The doctor obviously prospered, however, far more from his activities as a planter than as a doctor. Janet Schaw observed that there were some "very good Physicians" in Wilmington, "the best of whom is a Scotchman [Thomas Cobham] at whose house I have seen many of the first planters." Ministers did not fare as well on the social scale as other professional men. As James Iredell simply phrased it: "this Country is not very fond of parsons."[4] And North Carolina parsons would have agreed. In any case, for a professional man to become socially acceptable he first needed to acquire considerable property to provide him with an adequate income, and most ministers did not have incomes that allowed them any more than a comfortable living.

In writing to his father in England about his fiancée, James Iredell described Hannah Johnston's family as "without exception, the first in this country in every respect, and in none more distinguishingly than in possessing an uncommon share of good sense, and the more admired rules of conduct." The family's character came first, but Iredell did not hesitate to remark that Miss Johnston's "fortune too is a very genteel one, though I do not exactly know how much." His cousin, Henry Eustace McCulloh spoke of it with admiration and assured Iredell that "the sooner a young man married the better"; that is, "provided he had a competent income."[5] This alliance, indeed, brought Iredell into one of the "first families" of North Carolina. Samuel Johnston (Hannah's brother and head of the family) fitted all the qualifications of being a gentleman. A graduate of Yale, who had studied law under a prominent Edenton lawyer, Thomas Barker, he was accumulating a huge library. He continuously represented his county in the General

Hannah Johnston Iredell

Assembly in the 1760s and 1770s, was both the clerk of the Chowan court and the clerk of the Superior Court for the Albemarle counties, and served on St. Paul's vestry. Economically, he owned enough land and slaves to be considered wealthy.

St. Paul's Church, Edenton

Young Iredell, from an impoverished English family, also had connections — the reason why he was in North Carolina. He had two cousins and a great-uncle who were or had served on the governor's council, but only one of these relatives thought of North Carolina as his permanent home. Iredell's great-uncle, the speculator, Henry McCulloh, had already gone back to England and McCulloh's son, Henry Eustace McCulloh, was essentially an Englishman who occasionally lived in North Carolina. The McCullohs had started their careers as placemen (that is, they derived their living chiefly from political offices and privileges) and could be considered planters only because of their large landholdings, which they used for speculative purposes. In contrast, the Johnston family who had migrated at approximately the same time as the McCullohs and for the same reason — that Gabriel Johnston had been appointed governor — had decided to establish their roots in the colony; to make it their home. Although entitled to be called a "first family," none of the immediate Johnston relatives sat on that bastion of privilege in the colonies, the governor's council.

North Carolina's gentry (or "natural" leaders), for the most part, were only beginning to secure the stability and self-confidence needed for social acceptance in the late colonial period — at a time when the colony's population was rapidly growing. They found themselves challenged not only by upwardly mobile inhabitants but also by friends of either the crown or the royal governor, who saw a quick opportunity for wealth and advancement because of their political connections. Unlike Virginia's Council where families such as Byrds, Carters, and Burwells were continually represented, many members of the North Carolina Council were fairly recent arrivals. The majority had been born in Britain and had migrated to North Carolina in hopes of seeking their fortune, partly through political offices and partly through land speculation. Between 1763 and 1775, eight of the eighteen councillors serving during those years had started out as placemen, and five of those individuals still found their offices their chief source of income.[6] In 1766 Samuel Johnston observed that Martin Howard, one of the councillors in the 1770s, would "find some advocates for Liberty in this province as violent as those he fled from in Rhode Island."[7] Johnston had made this statement shortly after Howard's arrival and his appointment as chief justice. Three years later, Howard became a member of the council. Although Johnston and Howard apparently enjoyed friendly relations, the former probably made the above statement with not only the spirit of liberty in mind but also bitterness that another placeman had made it in North Carolina.

Several councillors (for instance, Howard) had not yet achieved great wealth. There were wealthier men in the colony at the time who did not sit on the council. Strangely absent in the Revolutionary Era were representatives of the old, aristocratic families who originally settled the Albemarle and Cape Fear regions. No men with the surname of Moore or Ashe, Swann or Harvey, served during those years — families which represented tradition, power, and wealth — although Moores and Swanns had served in earlier years. Albemarle representation on the council in the Revolutionary Era was practically non-existent.

The Moore family could hold its own with any representatives of the colonial aristocracy. Descendants of an early South Carolina governor, they migrated to the Cape Fear in the 1720s after one brother, Maurice Moore the elder, had previously helped North Carolina in the Tuscarora War and had married the daughter of Alexander Lillington, who was at the time the widow of Samuel Swann the elder. Upon the opening of the Cape Fear region to settlement, he and his brothers received extensive land grants. One brother, Roger, was referred to as "King Roger" because of his accumulation of lands in the area. A decade later, after their settlement, the family had already become renowned for their beautiful plantations — fine brick houses with commanding views on the Cape Fear River and its branches — and for their political power. When James Murray migrated to the colony in the late 1730s, he quickly sided with his patron, Governor Johnston, and incurred the wrath of the Moore family. He was "turned out" of the shop that he had rented from Roger Moore. Murray later became a member of the governor's council — a position that he served in until 1765, when he left the province. The Scottish shopkeeper (afterwards merchant) managed to obtain as high a position as his antagonist.[8]

Maurice Moore II, the son of the first Maurice Moore, held various political offices and was a recognized leader of the Lower Cape Fear. At the time that he served a brief stint on the governor's council, 1760 to 1761, he owned sixty-four slaves and two thousand acres of land — probably an underestimate of his wealth.[9] During the Revolutionary Era, he represented the town of Brunswick in the assembly every year until 1774. He was considered one of the legislative leaders because of committee assignments. In 1774 his nephew, Parker Quince, assumed Moore's seat. At the time that Moore was a member of the assembly, he was also an associate justice of the Superior Court, although he was removed in 1765 (but later restored) for his opposition to the Stamp Act. Nor was the governor understanding of Moore's later sympathy for the regulators. Moore's brother and brother-in-law, James Moore and John Ashe, continuously represented New Hanover County in the assembly in the 1760s and 1770s and his half-brother, Samuel Swann, represented Pasquotank County until the latter's death. A nephew, Robert Howe, represented Brunswick County. The Moores with their Ashe, Howe, Quince relatives dominated politics, lands, and slaves in the Lower Cape Fear region.

Although Maurice Moore only served a year on the council, another member of the family, a cousin, William Dry, sat on that august body from 1764 to 1775. One of the wealthiest members of the council, Dry on occasion espoused the radical cause. Miss Schaw found him, of all the Brunswick gentlemen, "the most zealous" in politics and noted that he "talks treason by the hour."[10] When the War for Independence broke out, Dry and the other four planters on the council stayed in the province; the placemen, the soldier and two merchants went home to England. The line was drawn between those who felt their strongest attachment to the home that they had created in North Carolina (in Dry's case, where he had been born) and those who could in no way deny their loyalty to the crown.

Just as in the Lower Cape Fear certain families dominated the political and social scene, other counties tended to elect continually the same men or members of the same families to represent them in the General Assembly and to serve as their local officials. Because the Albemarle counties sent more representatives to the assembly did not mean a loosening of family connections. In that region Harveys, Blounts, Joneses, Sawyers, Waltons, and Sumners monopolized local affairs. Perquimans County generally sent three Harveys to the assembly before the War for Independence broke out — two brothers and a son. The son had taken his father-in-law's position. Rowan County in the West followed suit and usually sent Griffith Rutherford, and Mecklenburg County continually sent Thomas Polk.

A major difference, though, existed between leading families of the East and families of the Piedmont. The eastern representatives generally came from families readily identified with the "Better Sort." Even though their fathers might have been self-made men, they had inherited their position and wealth and were only adding to their property. Their origins were known for the most part, and their families had established themselves as recognized leaders of the community. In the West many of the representatives came from obscure backgrounds and were themselves self-made men. They had moved into the Piedmont for the specific purpose of improving their economic status and were clearly men on the make. They had not yet acquired an aura of "genteel independency."

Thomas Polk, for instance, came from Cumberland County, Pennsylvania, and because of his pleasing manner and good education he became a representative from Mecklenburg County after it was formed from Anson County. Earlier, he had led Anson County settlers in the so-called War of Sugar Creek that was directed against the practices of land agent Henry Eustace McCulloh. A decade later, however, Polk stood by Tryon at Alamance. Griffith Rutherford, Rowan's favorite, came either from Pennsylvania or New Jersey. Little is known of his background, but he rose to prominence in Rowan. John Dunn, who sometimes represented the town of Salisbury, came from Maryland in the 1750s where he had been either a tenant farmer or an indentured servant. But in Salisbury he established a legal practice and became one of the justices of peace for the county. Dunn was obviously one of those "pettyfoggers" that Iredell's uncle had mentioned. But men like Polk, Rutherford, and Dunn settled down as insiders. Others stayed on the outside of the community.[11]

John Frohock, one of the wealthiest men on the frontier, and a representative from Rowan County in the 1760s, came from Pennsylvania in 1759 or

1760. In three years he accumulated at least six thousand acres of land in North Carolina including six grist or saw mills and several town lots in Halifax and Salisbury. By 1768 he had added two thousand more acres to his original holdings and owned thirty-eight slaves. Frohock could easily acquire good land because he was Henry Eustace McCulloh's surveyor and his relationship to McCulloh was further cemented by his brother's marrying McCulloh's cousin. Frohock not only invested in land, but he also accumulated political offices. Aside from being a representative in the assembly, he was clerk of the Rowan court from 1761 until his death in 1772. He was also the receiver of Rowan quitrents. During the regulator troubles, he was found guilty of fraud.[12]

The primary target of the regulators, however, was Edmund Fanning. Fanning, a graduate of Yale, had studied law in New York before journeying south to Orange County in 1761. He quickly became a representative in the General Assembly as well as the register of deeds, judge of the Superior Court and a colonel in the militia. He appeared a leader and qualified as a "gentleman"; yet he had only been in Orange County a short time, and as far as the regulators were concerned, he was prospering by charging illegal and excessive fees — clearly not in the interest of the public. An imaginary conversation between Fanning and Frohock in a regulator ballad shows some of the antipathy felt for men of their ilk:

Says Frohawk to Fanning, to tell the plain truth,
When I came to this country I was but a youth:
My father sent for me; I wa'nt worth a cross,
And then my first study was to cheat for a horse.
I quickly got credit and strait ran away,
And Hav'nt paid for him to this very day.

Says Fanning to Frohawk, 'tis a folly to lie,
I rode on an old mare that was bline of one eye,
Six shillings in money I had in my purse,
My coat it was patch'd but not much the worse.
But now we've got rich, and 'tis very well known
That we'll do well enough if they'll let us alone.[13]

The regulators and their sympathizers obviously had not yet ascribed a spirit of *noblesse oblige* to these two men.

The courthouse cliques dominated by certain families apparently ran affairs in all the counties, but in the West they appeared a crasser, much more vulgar group in their operations than did their peers in the East. The Moravians found it unpleasant to attend court "because conduct there is so ungodly." Their description of one of the Rowan justices — that the court "was very noisy, for [Edward] Hughes defended the man" — might give some impression of local government or attitudes towards it. The same Hughes had earlier been sheriff of Rowan County and had been charged with fraud after he had left office. Neither did individuals show any respect on election days, when there was always the problem of voter sobriety. A young lawyer newly settled in Rowan County in describing a 1769 election day in Tryon County "heard much caballing; saw much bruising, Goughling & Biting."[14]

North Carolinians, especially those in the West, suffered from too much local government. Tryon estimated that there were "five hundred and sixteen acting justices in the province which consists of only twenty nine counties." But the main representative and symbol of local government was the sheriff, one of the best paid colonial officials but frequently one of the most corrupt. Aside from regular fees, he received a commission (from 6 to 8 per cent) for collecting parish, county, and colony taxes. All counties at one time or another had a corrupt sheriff, but the newer, western-most counties by far had the greatest number. In those five counties which had all been established at mid-century or after, there were twenty-nine "errant sheriffs." Also in those counties there was a much wider discrepancy between arrears and collections. "When Tryon succeeded in 1769 in having a thorough accounting made of the colony's finances, a delinquency on the part of the sheriffs was found which amounted to £64,000, £3,000 more than the total taxes collected in the period 1748-1770." Members of the assembly had done nothing about the local graft — doubtless because of their connections with the sheriff who was a powerful figure in local politics. The assemblymen were generally justices of the peace and relied on the sheriff for support back home — especially on election day.[15]

The eastern political leaders, then, allied themselves with western politicians who were oftentimes accused of corruption and were, in some instances, considered outsiders in the community. But the latter provided the political and social leadership that was required in a society that was not highly centralized. When the eastern gentlemen looked at the rapidly growing West, they saw not only a land of opportunity but also a haven for debtors and criminals. The assembly was blind to the corrupt acts of county officials, but it believed that a number of criminals inhabited the colony, especially in the West: horsethieves, hogthieves, counterfeiters, bandits, and gamblers. Perhaps North Carolina gentlemen had talked to the Moravians who were frequently the victims of theft or reported various crimes in their neighborhood. Or assemblymen could simply look at the county records which indicated a variety of petty crimes, and some felonies. Waightstill Avery, shortly after beginning his law practice, won a verdict of not guilty for a man charged with petty larceny. Almost immediately he "was surrounded with a flood of Clients" who wanted him to defend them. In the end, he took thirty cases for that term.[16]

In maintaining the social order certain institutions played a dominant role in the eighteenth century: the government, representative of the civil establishment; the church, representative of spiritual authority; and the family, society's basic unit. In varying degree colonials supported these institutions. North Carolina's royal government faced several difficulties, however, as a centralizing agency. Maintaining law and order was only one problem. The fact that approximately half of the colony's lands lay in the Granville District did not help the colony financially and weakened central authority.* In addition the Granville land office had closed in the early 1760s which precluded the further issuance of grants, and the government could not open the office. Other administrative problems also existed. No permanent capital was established until 1765, so that one could not pinpoint the government's location. Its papers were moving by cart from Wilmington to Edenton to New Bern — wherever the assembly was meeting. The people in the West, grossly under-represented in the assembly, had more dealings with their local government than the central unit and cared little whether a capital was established or whether the necessary buildings were constructed. Their suspicions of local politicians, of course, did not encourage an unquestioning loyalty to public officials in general. In addition, western farmers had few economic ties with the East which could have cemented political ties. They sold their surplus crops mainly to either local factors or Charles Town or Virginia merchants. Those markets were more important to their economic well-being than the business transacted in North Carolina maritime towns.

The Church of England in North Carolina, although established by law, was also weak. There were few priests, especially before Tryon's administration, and parish taxes were not regularly collected. In parishes where dissenters constituted the majority of the population, vestries would not take office, which not only undermined the position of the Anglican church but also poor relief. In the 1760s the assembly pushed by Governor Tryon put the church on a sounder foundation. There were probably Presbyterian members of the assembly who voted for the vestry acts of the 1760s simply because they saw the possibility of the church's becoming a centralizing force and thereby strengthening the social order. In return, Tryon singled out the Presbyterians for special favors and gained their support during the War of the Regulation. The Baptists doubtless believed that the Presbyterians had sold their souls to the government. In general, however, all dissenters, including Presbyterians (and even some Anglicans) saw little or no need for an established church. Neither government nor church, then, effectively centralized North Carolina society. The institution of the family, however, was strong; nevertheless it did not always serve as a centralizing agency. The closest ties that many North Carolinians had were with their

---

*Earl Granville retained his proprietary rights to Carolina when the other proprietors sold their shares to the crown. He and his heirs held the land rights to one-eighth of the territory of Carolina as it was in 1663. The area set aside for Granville was approximately the northern half of North Carolina, which comprised the wealthiest and most populated section of the colony.

families, especially since the population was scattered. But families did not identify as much with the colony or state as with their local communities and their local church congregations. A number of North Carolinians (because of language barriers) could only converse with their relatives or members of their church congregations. They were left out of the main-stream of society. A man from Nutbush, when asked who he was, might very well reply a resident of Nutbush (Granville County) — not a Carolinian; let alone a British-American.

In the face of the inherent divisiveness in North Carolina society, the Establishment also witnessed a leveling influence, which undermined dele-gated authority. The very nature of the ethnic and religious diversity of the population produced a leveling effect. Because residents accepted the dif-ferences of their neighbors, a spirit of toleration existed. Individuals living on isolated farms easily recognized the worth of the individual and appreci-ated human contact. They particularly appreciated the local ordinary (or tavern) not only as a place of relaxation but also as a source of information where one could learn about happenings in the outside world.

An English visitor in 1774 described Jethro Sumner who later became a general of the American army as being a "lusty, and rather handsome" person "with an easy and genteel address" who had been a captain in the French and Indian War; but that which "contributed more to his appoint-ment and promotion in the American Army, than any other merit" was "his violent principles, and [his] keeping an inn at the courthouse (which is scarcely thought a mean occupation here), singular as the latter circum-stance may appear."[17]

The "Better Sort" themselves contributed to the freer social situation not only by associating with innkeepers but by the informality of manners in public meetings. In 1787 a visitor remarked that the members of the assembly all kept on their hats during session except when they spoke. He had already faced a similar situation when he had had breakfast. He had removed his hat "without any ceremony" and had taken his "seat amongst the Crowd; Legislators, Planters and Merchants. After being all seated I lifted up my eyes and saw that I had committed a faux pas, every Man but me had kept his Hat on." Whether legislators observed the same custom earlier remains unknown, but James Murray when he opened his store in the 1730s easily sold all his products but his wigs. He found no market at all for wigs; nor did it develop. He mentioned one of the reasons as being the wear-ing of hats. All such habits led Janet Schaw to find "a most disgusting equality" in North Carolina society. She still had hopes, however, to meet an "American Gentleman." She was positive the breed existed.[18]

It is little wonder, then, that when the regulator movement broke out, the eastern Establishment saw society itself disintegrating. At a time when

Lord Granville

they were trying to become a civilized and cohesive community — to improve the position of the church and to establish the government in one location — the farmers in the Piedmont were demonstrating how loosely structured North Carolina society was. And, thus, the "natural leaders" joined Governor Tryon without hesitation to put down the rebellion. They believed that mob violence could easily lead to anarchy. No doubt some of them remembered the early history of the colony when chaos had sometimes prevailed. This is not to say that the movement was a class conflict as such. But the elite feared the disruption of the social order, while the regulators, many of them prosperous farmers, could not make the Establishment understand the evils that existed in their local government.

Various interpretations have been advanced to explain the regulator movement, which range from sectional and class explanations to the identification of the movement with the struggle for independence. But the most plausible explanations always center around the grievances that the westerners held against the local courthouse rings. The rebellion clearly broke out as a dispute over taxation. Ironically, individuals in Granville, Orange, Rowan and Anson counties were objecting, often violently, to the high fees charged by local officials, the oppressive poll taxes, and the onerous methods used by sheriffs to collect those taxes at the same time as members of the assembly were protesting parliamentary taxation under the Stamp and Townshend Acts.

North Carolina suffered from much heavier taxation after 1755; partly because of expenses incurred by the French and Indian War and partly because of increasing governmental expenditures due to the rapid growth of the colony. But the most controversial expenditure was the construction of the Governor's Palace. The heavier taxes also came at a time when there was little currency in the colony. In the East, warehouse receipts, given after the inspection of indigo and tobacco, could be used for tax payment, but there were few warehouses in the West. Nor could farmers pay their taxes in commodities — the only kind of payment that they could really afford. To make the situation worse, many westerners justifiably questioned whether their taxes were ending up in the public treasury or were subsidizing corrupt sheriffs. They saw their property being distrained if they could not make immediate payment and being sold at a much lower price than it was worth. Then, in 1768, the sheriffs were enabled to set up certain collection points where taxes were to be paid. If a man did not pay his taxes there, the sheriff could charge extra for a private collection.

Herman Husband, if not one of the leaders of the regulator movement, at lease an ardent sympathizer, wrote that at the same time as the sheriff of Orange County announced designated places for tax collection came also "the Rumour of giving the Governor *Fifteen Thousand Pounds,* to build him a House" which together "conspired to give Rise to what was commonly called the Mob; which in a little Time altered to that of the Regulators." In their fourth "Advertisement" written in the spring of 1768, the regulators declared that they would "pay no Taxes until we are satisfied they are agreeable to Law"; in addition, they would elect better men to office and would petition the government for a redress of grievances. In June, Governor Tryon reported that the riots had subsided and he was certain that if the crown granted the colony permission to print some more paper money "the public taxes would be collected without any obstruction."[19]

But the associations did not cease, and Edmund Fanning, instead of negotiating with the regulators over their grievances as he had promised, ordered the arrest of William Butler, one of the leaders, and Herman Husband, who was not actually in the association but who had been appointed by the regulators as one of their mediators. As a result 700 men marched on Hillsborough to liberate the prisoners. The county officials quickly released them, but agitation still continued and spread to other counties. Tryon, in hopes of quieting the disturbances, decided to go to Hillsborough in July. He called out the militia to accompany him in order to protect the Superior Court, which would be meeting at that time to try Butler and Husband. Although many men refused to serve, over 1,000 soldiers (20 per cent of them officers) accompanied the governor, and the regulators did not disrupt the court proceedings. The court acquitted Husband but found three "insurgents" guilty and ordered them imprisoned and fined. Tryon, however, suspended the sentence. The court also found Fanning guilty of extortion. He had purportedly been misinformed about the law and had not realized that he was charging illegal fees. After paying a small fine he immediately resigned as register of deeds. Tryon once more assured the crown that the agitation was over and "not a person of the character of a gentleman appeared among the insurgents."[20]

The regulators waited to see if their grievances would be redressed and elected Herman Husband as a representative from Orange County to take the place of Edmund Fanning. In nearby Rowan County, the people elected another regulator sympathizer, Matthew Locke, and in Granville County they elected the man often referred to as "the wealthy Regulator," Thomas Person. But the associations found the legislative machinery slow and before any lasting reforms could be instituted, the governor dissolved the assembly because of its opposition to the Townshend duties.

In September, 1770, the regulators once more took matters in their own hands, marched on Hillsborough, "assembled together in the Court Yard" and "insulted some of the Gentlemen of the Bar, & in a violent manner went into the court house, and forceably carried out some of the attorneys, and in a cruel manner beat them." They asked Judge Richard Henderson to "proceed to the Tryal of their Leaders, who had been indicted at a former court, and that the Jury should be taken out of their party." Judge Henderson, thoroughly frightened, managed to survive, and having decided "to break up Court than sit and be made a mock Judge for the sport and entertainment of those Abandoned Wretches," made his escape.

The *Virginia Gazette* reported that,

> When they had full glutted their revenges on the lawyers, and particularly Colonel Fanning, to show their opinion of courts of justice they took from his chains a negro that had been executed some time, and placed him at the lawyer's bar, and filled the Judge's seat with human excrement, in derision and contempt of the charac-

ters that fill those respectable places. Would a Hottentot have been guilty of such a piece of brutality?

It is little wonder that some of the Orange County officials wrote to Tryon that the rioters were "a set of Men ... whom We have long considered as dangerous to Society, and as pursuing every Measure destructive of Peace and good Government." They believed that this incident "proved, that they only want Time, and a larger Body of their disaffected Tools of Faction, to effect purposes of the most dangerous and dismal Tendency and which We apprehend must ... end in the Ruin and Destruction of the Province."[21]

Both the assembly and the governor in the December session of 1770 expressed sympathy for the grievances of the regulators — enough so for James Iredell to write John Harvey that "no Fees whatever are to be allowed — the Lawyers are to be scourged too — In short, it seems that a majority of the houses are of regulating Principles." But the assembly did retaliate against the violence after hearing that the regulators intended to march on New Bern. They passed the Johnston Act in January, 1771, which declared that "any Persons" who had engaged in a riotous assembly "to the Number of ten or more" and had been ordered dispersed by "one or more Justices of the Peace or Sheriff" would "be adjudged Felons and shall suffer Death." The act, to be in effect for one year, was also made *ex post facto* to include all riots since March, 1770.[22] Disturbances, nevertheless, continued despite the act; grand juries began to bring in indictments. Tryon once more had the opportunity to call out troops and could this time stamp out the regulators. Again the governor had difficulty in recruiting from the rank and file, but the assembly (many of them militia officers) fully supported his actions. Fourteen per cent of the men were officers — many of them from the eastern aristocracy, who were making their protests against royal government at the same time as the regulators were protesting local government.

Was the War of the Regulation, then, a social or class revolution? Governor Tryon appreciated the fact that no gentlemen were involved, and the eastern elite were certainly opposed to the upheaval. But there were wealthy men on the side of the regulators — some of them residents of the community longer than the people they opposed. True, the regulators called themselves poor men, but they did not place themselves in opposition to wealthy men *per se*. In an Orange County petition they expressed their desire to be taxed "in proportion to" their estates. They noted that on the frontier very few men held slaves, which were included in a poll tax. Wealthy slaveholders, thus, primarily in the East, paid the most taxes in the colony. But there were individuals in the Piedmont with large amounts of land, whose "Estates are in proportion (in many instances) as of one Thousand to one," who held few slaves or not any at all. Yet they paid the same taxes as a man with less land: "for all to pay equal, is with Submission, very grievous and oppressive." The Orange County petitioners realized that the eastern gentry paid more taxes because of their slaveholdings; they also knew that some wealthy westerners paid the same amount of taxes as the average or poor farmer did. What they wanted then was to establish a more equitable basis for taxation in the West.[23]

Many of the reforms requested by the Anson regulators involved election as well as tax abuses. They wanted the vote given "by Ticket and Ballot." Besides a close regulation of fees and the setting of fixed salaries for officials, they also wanted taxes to be paid in produce and the building of warehouses in the Piedmont which would accordingly issue warehouse receipts, which could be used as paper money. In addition to these reforms, the various petitioners wanted to see a new system devised for the granting of lands. Both governors Tryon and Martin agreed that the methods (or lack of methods) by which land was acquired contributed to the disturbances. In the early 1760s the Granville land office had closed, which necessitated thereafter a person's going to county officials if he wanted land. The Anson County residents were not troubled as much by the Granville office as by Henry McCulloh's methods of distributing land; one of the reasons why Frohock was disliked so much and charged with fraud. All of these demands were reasonable. What the regulators wanted, in short, was responsible government, and at first they had been quite willing to work within the system.[24]

"All we want is to be Governed by Law," wrote Herman Husband, "and not by the *Will* of Officers, which to us is perfectly despotick and arbitrary . . . it is but seldom these Gentry will condescend to tell us what is Law, but, *Pay me so much Money,* is their usual manner of accosting us; and if we say, we will not pay until we know what it is for, away goes the horse to the Post, for sale, or the man to Prison; though the latter is seldom the case; that not being the way to enrich the Tax-gatherer." Husband believed that the colony had become an asylum for a group of politicians, many of them in New Bern, who possessed no religion or moral obligation. In contrast, the main body of Orange County residents, migrants from the North, were "good industrious labouring Men; who knew the value of their property better than to let it go to enrich, Pettyfogging Lawyers."[25]

In another account, Husband reminded his readers "that a majority of our Assembly is composed of Lawyers, clerks, and others in connection with them, while by our own Voice we have excluded the Planter." The people could not expect such a group to pass legislation favorable to "the Farmer, and consequently of the community" — a group "whose highest Study is the Promotion of their Wealth." While such statements could be used to support a class conflict interpretation, Husband is not including true gentlemen in his list of scoundrels. What is involved is a view of whether an agrarian society should be governed by its own leaders (planters) who would be responsible to their constituents or by new arrivals (especially lawyers and clerks) who felt little responsibility for their constituents and did not appreciate the values of the community; who only wanted to control its political affairs and to make their financial investments pay off.[26]

Many regulators were substantial farmers in their communities. In Granville County the regulators owned as much property as the average taxpayer in the county, and individual regulators owned quite a bit more land. The taxpayers (from a random sampling of the tax list) owned an average of 314 acres per individual while the regulators averaged 315 acres. In number of acres held, the mean for the control group (taxpayers selected randomly) was 1,134 acres; for the regulators, 2,168 acres. The regulators who held land owned 130 acres more per person than the average landowner in the county. Of course, 60 per cent of the control group owned land whereas only 48 per cent of the regulators did, which in part meant that those regulators who owned land held larger amounts than the control group. The regulators also had settled in the county earlier than the control group and had acquired most of their land before the closing of the land office. There appeared to be a rivalry between the older settlers (who became regulators) and some of the new arrivals (who joined the courthouse ring) in obtaining the best properties.[27] All of this information would give credence to the belief that county officials who clearly did not have the best interest of the community at heart encouraged the discontent of the local residents. If they had exercised their authority with more discretion and more *noblesse oblige,* they might have kept control of the people without any serious outbreaks of violence, as the eastern political leaders managed to do. Members of the courthouse rings, men such as Edmund Fanning, had taken full advantage of the economic opportunities and the new value system (economic democracy) especially offered by the rapidly growing western counties. They had "made" it, but once they had achieved success, they returned to the old value system based on unquestioning deference to one's "betters." The regulators did not mind that men became wealthy through honest labor or that wealthy men governed, but they resented the dishonesty practiced by local public officials and their lack of governmental responsibility. In the regulator view, political leaders were to govern for the public welfare. Only then should they enjoy the community's appreciation or respect for their contributions.

Governor Martin sympathized with the regulator grievances after his tour of the West in 1772. He clearly saw that they had "been provoked by insolence and cruel advantages taken of the peoples ignorance by mercenary tricking Attorneys, Clerks and other little Officers who have practiced upon them every sort of rapine and extortion by which having brought upon themselves their just resentment they engaged Government in their defence by artful misrepresentation."[28] Governor Martin could see what the eastern Establishment could not. In choosing sides, they saw local political (and, hence, social) leadership being challenged and the disruption of a social order that they were trying to develop. They could not suffer that kind of behavior in a civilized society. Ironically they allied themselves with the royal governor, and, in essence, placemen, whom the easterners identified as gentlemen but who had little regard for the community interest. In the regulator mind, on the other hand, the eastern gentlemen had become suspect by allying themselves with western speculators and extortioners.

Under the pseudonym of Atticus, Judge Maurice Moore saw some of the irony of the situation. He criticized Tryon's handling of the whole regulator affair and traced it back to the taxes needed for the Governor's Palace; that "the Infant and impoverished State of this Country could not afford to make such a Grant." Yet, the assembly had been led into this "Mischief" by the governor, who, then, "regardless of every moral as well as legal Obligation, changed the Plan of the Province House for that of a Palace" that was fit for a prince. The public imposition for the structure, as far as Moore was concerned, had led to the "Civil War," and Tryon, if he had really acted like a responsible governor, could have avoided the crisis of 1768 by acting less hastily in calling out the troops.[29]

The judge also criticized the Riot Act and pointed out its unconstitutionality. Following up on that criticism, Moore ruled in 1772 that the court would seek no further prosecutions under that act. At the close of his public letter to Governor Tryon, printed in the *Virginia Gazette,* Moore mentioned a scene at a recent ball in which he believed that the governor had shown a remarkable "Littleness of Mind," which "when blended with the Dignity and Importance of his office render him Truly ridiculous."[30] Maurice Moore II proved himself a truly responsible member of the community and a gentleman whether any of his peers did or not.

At Alamance, the "Better Sort," in their view, had saved the province from anarchy and had strengthened civilized society. By 1776 they had established their leadership and were growing in power. But the Revolution, which they had encouraged, once the provisional government had been set up and the fighting had started, began to undermine the prestige and power that they had achieved. The regulator movement had initially caused people to think about responsible government and to question authority. The War for Independence gave them the opportunity to express themselves once more; but this time, they had the opportunity to create a new government based on republican principles. How much power the people should have, and in what ways it should be checked immediately became pressing issues.

Samuel Johnston had assumed the revolutionary leadership after the death of John Harvey in 1775 and led the colony into rebellion against the mother country. But by the fall of 1776 Johnston had become too conservative for the radical element of the revolutionary party led by Willie Jones and Thomas Person. In the bitterly fought election of 1776 — one in which Johnston was burned in effigy — the radicals managed to defeat him and thus prevented his attending as a delegate the provincial congress that would draft and approve the new state constitution. James Iredell, in an angry mood over the results of the election, jotted down his sentiments, which he entitled "Creed of a Rioter," a somewhat exaggerated revelation of Iredell's belief that class antagonism had caused Johnston's defeat. The first principle of a rioter, according to Iredell, was the belief that all gentlemen were his enemies, and that no gentleman could "possibly possess either honor or virtue." Iredell, of course, believed the opposite was true, and the election of 1776 and its aftermath caused both him and Johnston to reflect about the declining power of the "natural leaders" — or the "Better Sort" — and the future of the province.[31]

Johnston attended the provincial congress that fall as an observer and was thankful that he was not a member. He witnessed proceedings in which he believed that "no one appears to have sufficient spirit or authority to set them right." As far as he was concerned, "every one who has the least pretensions to be a gentleman is suspect and borne down *per ignobile vulgis* — a set of men without reading, experience, or principle to govern them." Johnston saw the convention draft a constitution that allowed greater participation in politics by providing for a generous suffrage — taxpayers and fifty acre freeholders could vote respectively for members of the House of Commons and the Senate — and relatively low requirements for officeholding — ownership of 100 acres for assemblymen and 300 acres for senators. The constitution also reflected the regulator influence by providing for a close supervision of public monies, fixed salaries for government offices, and restrictions against multiple officeholding. No religious group was to have preferred treatment.[32]

The document was by far the most democratic of all the state constitutions with the exception of Pennsylvania's. It is little wonder that Johnston called it the work "of men without reading, experience, or principle." On the other hand, the document was not all that radical. For instance, it did not provide for proportional representation, and it did not have to be submitted to the people for ratification.

In the late 1770s and the 1780s the North Carolina Senate reflected the democratic trend in the new state. Whereas only eighteen men had served on the governor's council in the years 1763 to 1775, over 250 senators were elected in the years 1776 to 1788. The council had been men of the "Better Sort," or at least they identified with that group; but substantial farmers could qualify for membership in the state Senate, and many of them did — some from obscure or humble backgrounds. Only 18 per cent of the members could be considered wealthy (on the basis of their owning fifty or more slaves) while 48 per cent could be called well-to-do (on the basis of their owning between twenty and fifty slaves). The remaining 34 per cent fell into the moderate range. Since senators had to own 300 acres, doubtless none could be classified as poor, but in comparison with the members of upper houses in other states, they approached that classification. In another breakdown of their socioeconomic status, 20 per cent of the senators came

44

from wealthy land-owning families, had taken an active part in the war and were knowledgeable of affairs outside the colony; 25 per cent represented lesser planters whose fathers had been established farmers in the colonial period; 25 per cent were themselves farmers of moderate means who had either migrated to the state or had come from local, generally humble origins. Thirty per cent were "remarkable only for their anonymity."[33]

The members of the House of Commons came from an even more varied background than did the senators. "Among the nearly one hundred men who voted several times during the sessions from 1783 to 1787 were six merchants, seven lawyers, six following some other nonfarm occupation, twenty-seven large landowners, and twenty-five farmers, the remaining twenty-eight being unknown." Only 15 per cent of the assemblymen could be considered wealthy; 32 per cent, well-to-do.[34] The leveling influence that observers noted in the years before the war had become apparent in the war-time and postwar legislative bodies. The leaders of the legislature, however, still continued to be from prominent families. The first state Senate elected Samuel Ashe its speaker; the House of Commons chose Abner Nash.

Conservative gentlemen generally agreed that they were losing influence, and many, like Johnston, retired briefly from the political arena in the early 1780s. Not all retired, however, and a spirit of factiousness existed throughout the 1780s in which the conservatives (later Federalists) were led by members of the old aristocracy. Prominent, wealthy men also led the radical group, but they had given up (if they had had any) their elitist assumptions, at least publicly. According to the conservatives, however, the radical leaders used the prejudices of the people for their own ends. The condescending attitudes of the elitists, however, hardly helped their cause. In 1783 Iredell wrote to his wife that the town of Hillsborough had not elected William Hooper. "It was owing, I am told, to the imprudence of some of his friends, who said something that gave offence to the common people, such as that a drink of toddy would easily bring them over."[35]

Not all gentlemen were so disparaging in their remarks. A German traveller (to show "what dignity a North Carolina justice demanded") related a story about a boxing match that took place in front of the house of a justice of the peace. The justice and his wife had both ordered the boxers to stop, but they would not. The justice could not command obedience "and was of the opinion that it was more in keeping with his official worth to pass over an apparent slight, instead of taking the proud revenge which an injured self-love might demand." William Attmore, who later discovered that North Carolinians wore their hats to both breakfast and the legislature, where they took them off only to speak, was amazed at the living conditions of one recent representative, John Bonner, whose family had laid out the town of Washington, North Carolina: "This Man tho' a Member of the Assembly, and a rich Batchelor, lived in an old house that had four Windows in the lower room only one of which appeared ever to have been glazed: the others had sash lights but no Glass."[36]

John Wright Stanly House

If North Carolina had been destined to become a more aristocratic society before the War for Independence, that trend had clearly been halted. The people had a larger voice in their government; their leaders could not thus ignore them. With a little talent, luck, and good hard labor, any man could improve his socioeconomic position, as before the war. Now he was even more assured that no privileged group would stand in his way. The traveller, William Attmore, met Jonathan Wright Stanly in New Bern, whom he had known earlier as a prisoner (for debt) in the Philadelphia jail. Stanly had moved to North Carolina "where by a Series of fortunate events in Trade during the War he acquired a great property, and has built a house in Newbern ... that is truly elegant and convenient; at an expense of near 20,000 Dollars." Aside from "a large Wharff and Distillery near his house," Stanly also had "a fine plantation with sixty Slaves thereon."[37] Stanly's rapid rise in society demonstrated the ease with which a capable individual could still acquire a fortune in North Carolina and then use that fortune to maintain his social position. Stanly himself had married Richard Cogdell's daughter, and their home became a center for New Bern social life. Not many men climbed the socioeconomic ladder as rapidly as Stanly. Not all men even desired to become members of the elite; on the other hand, they did not question whether men should be socially equal. Most North Carolinians recognized that there were social classes; that some men naturally belonged to an elite group that furnished the leaders for the community. But most

North Carolinians did demand equality before the law and wanted economic democracy; the chance to make their own fortunes.

Although some of the names of the elite had changed by the 1780s as prosperous farmers became wealthy planters or new arrivals made their fortunes, the upper class or "Better Sort" still provided social and political leadership for the community or the state; even the leaders of the radicals were men of property. The latter had simply given up their elitist assumptions with respect to the purposes of government and how it should be operated. They respected public opinion and they demanded that the rights of the individual should be protected; they thus held out for a Bill of Rights in the federal Constitution. But they did not deny the existence of class lines. A somewhat exaggerated view of Willie Jones, the leader of the Antifederalists, saw him as "ultra-democratic in theory," but "aristocratic in habits, tastes, pursuits and prejudices: he lived sumptuously, and wore fine linen; he raced, hunted, and played cards; he was proud of his wealth, and social position; and fastidious in the selection of associates for his family."[38] Willie Jones found it possible to maintain the social order; even in an increasingly democratic society of his own making.

By the late 1780s, Samuel Johnston was once more engaged in politics; first as a legislator, then governor, and president of the ratifying convention for the federal Constitution. The people of Chowan had been restored "to a lucid interval," according to William Hooper, and had given thought to "their future society."[39] The "natural" leaders only had to wait to be called on by their constituents. The yeomen of North Carolina had wrested power from the "natural" leaders, but they also were willing to give that power back. The farmers symbolized North Carolina society; their values permeated that society. But there was still an inherent consciousness that men of the "Better Sort" should lead; albeit they should also be scrupulously watched.

CHAPTER III

NORTH CAROLINIANS AT HOME

The traveller visiting North Carolina in the late eighteenth century journeyed through "a continuous, measureless forest, an ocean of trees." He found a variety of roads from the very good (to his surprise) to the barely passable. In some places he ran the risk of entirely losing his way (especially at night) due to the density of the woods. Along the road were milestones or posts "with the Number of Miles marked on them in Roman Numerals, & as many Notches cut in the Side of it as you have Miles to travel ... for the Benefit of the unlearned," decided one Pennsylvanian. Here and there, the traveller found "cultivated spots, what are called plantations. ... scattered about in these woods at various distances, 3-6 miles, and often as much as 10-15-20 miles apart." In the middle of the fields stood "a house, better or worse; the kitchen and other mean out-buildings ... at a distance." Along the way one might also find an isolated tavern (or ordinary), a countrystore at a busy crossroads — or a small town dominated by a courthouse and church and bustling with people if on a court day or an election day. If late at night, the traveller looked for a house with candles beaming through the windows. Or, if he were caught in a rainstorm, the nearest shelter, little better than a small log cabin, could suddenly become a palace.[1]

Most travellers preferred to stay in homes rather than try their luck at an unknown ordinary. As one New Englander noted (and with praise for southern hospitality), "travellers with any pretensions to respectability, seldom stop at the wretched taverns; but custom sanctions their freely calling at any planter's residence." At a tavern, one might find that he had an uninvited bed partner the next morning when he woke up. Or, even when he went to bed, he might have to share the mattress with his travelling companions. William Attmore was thankful that at Mrs. Cobb's "petty ordinary" each man had his own clean bed. The eighty-three year old woman's "house consisted of two apartments one was the sitting Room, the floor was of Clay or dirt, and there was one Bed in the Room." But the guest room "was floored with Boards and contained four good Beds." The food was only adequate, but the horses were well provided.[2]

Tavern fare, indeed, did not always excite the traveller's palate: "old geese, suckling pigs and raw salad, there being no vinegar," remarked a German visitor disparagingly. Pork, bacon, cornbread, and greens could generally be expected. Most travellers enjoyed meals served at some farmer's home much better than "Ordinary" food. A Frenchman feasted "on

48

venison stakes in a poor farmers house" near Bath. He found bacon, however, as "the Chief suport of all the Inhabitants, when fishing is out of season. it is a Dainty Dish here tho ever so fat or rare." At another farmer's house in the Albemarle region, he enjoyed "good fat Bacon, greens and Indian bread and had good sider." Beverages were always available in quantity, and the amount of rum sold by country stores and taverns still excites the imagination of historians. William Attmore noted with some surprise that "it is very much the custom in North Carolina to drink Drams of some kind or other before Breakfast; sometimes Gin, Cherry-bounce, Egg Nog." On Christmas day, he emphasized that he had had egg nog — and with rum — for breakfast.[3]

Travellers used a variety of adjectives to describe North Carolinians and the way they lived: slovenly and ignorant; lazy and indolent; inquisitive and rude yet hospitable; robust and sickly; lusty and attractive; gaunt and raw-boned. Differences in opinion can be explained in part by the variety of personalities encountered by visitors — a cross-section of society. The frequent references to the indolence and crudeness of North Carolina residents stemmed partially from the observations of genteel visitors who often met individuals whom they considered inferior in social status and with whom, under ordinary circumstances, they would have had little association. As a Spanish adventurer phrased it: "their social system is still in a state of infancy." J. F. D. Smyth covered the social spectrum (and the accompanying adjectives) in his visit to North Carolina in 1774. In trying to find directions near Chowan Sound, he "called at several miserable hovels, at the distances of five or six miles asunder, but could neither obtain directions on my way, or any kind of refreshment." The "ignorant wretches" advised him to go to Mr. Tyers's "for he often had strange, outlandish folks to lodge at his house and was a rich man, and had a mill, and a blacksmith's shop, and a still." The Englishman found "these people . . . the most wretchedly ignorant of any I ever met with. They could not tell me the name of the place, country or parish they resided in." Smyth finally found Mr. Tyers, "the only magistrate in this place for thirty miles around, and . . . the only intelligent being." The visitor also found his house "the seat of plenty and plainness, mirth and good-humour, and genuine hospitality without ostentation; but entirely out of the way from all public roads."[4]

The latter description underscored the nature of North Carolina society — even what determined a man's wealth in the popular image. North Carolinians enjoyed lush natural surroundings, but they built their houses simply and lived with little ostentation. "Tolerable dwelling," the term sometimes used in newspaper advertisements, gives a hint of the simplicity and practicality demanded by residents, as well as the middle-class nature of society. North Carolina's architecture reflected the variety of backgrounds of its citizens. Domestic styles ranged from the humble one-room

Samuel Johnston's Hayes Plantation

log cabin to the Stanly home described by William Attmore as the most elegant house in New Bern. The latter, built about 1770, resembled some of the Hudson River mansions, and its parlors reflected a Philadelphia influence.[5] The log house in the Piedmont, although it did not resemble any Philadelphia parlors, also owed its appearance to Pennsylvania architecture. Other small, frame houses owed their design to British styles. Many Carolinians born in England or Scotland were accustomed to small cottages, which contained one room for living, a sleeping loft, and one room used as a stable. Once the British moved to the New World, they simply removed the stable from the living quarters, and sometimes they built a separate kitchen.

Only towards the end of the colonial period were planters beginning to build structures that one readily identifies with southern plantations. In Wilmington, New Bern, and Edenton visitors usually noted that the houses were small, sometimes "indifferent," frame, but comfortable. If he had come from Virginia or Charles Town, a traveller probably did find the homes of North Carolina planters and merchants small in comparison with their neighbors. But one also found the Charles Town influence in the building of "Balconies or Piazzas in front and sometimes back of the house, this method of Building is found convenient on account of the great Summer Heats here." Some houses reflected a truly Georgian style, especially after the arrival of John Hawks, the English builder of Tryon's Palace. But few planters used brick. Perhaps it was because nobody thought "himself rich enough to live in a brick house" — the reason offered by one visitor why nobody would buy Tryon's Palace during the 1780s. Although the Moores and their relatives (perhaps with a note of their status as well as their intended permanency) had used brick in the 1730s, visitors described most of the houses of the Lower Cape Fear as frame. The same was true of the Albemarle region, as well as in the Piedmont. Apparently not until 1782 did a western resident, Colonel John Johnston (Samuel Johnston's brother), build a brick house west of the Catawba River.[6]

For most North Carolinians their first home was a log cabin, often with earthen floors and unglazed window openings that were enclosed in stormy weather by a swinging shutter. Windows were small, whether with or without glass. A large opening might be no more than one foot five inches by two feet four inches; while a small window could measure seven inches by twelve inches. The cabin, dominated by the fireplace at one end, generally contained only one room in its primitive condition; perhaps, in size, twenty-four feet by eighteen feet. Logs could not conveniently exceed twenty-four feet in house building so that a number of early homes are either of that length, or smaller. If the owner prospered, he could then add an extra room as well as wooden floors; perhaps even a hall between the two rooms or a "dog-run" with a stairs that would lead to the upper floor. In many cabins only a ladder allowed entrance to the sleeping loft, which would then be used by children and servants. The more sophisticated structure with only one room would have a narrow winding stairs to one side of the fireplace.[7]

Governor Tryon wrote "that the poorer Settlers coming from the North-ward Colonies sat themselves down in the back Counties where the land is the best but who have not more than a sufficiency to erect a Log House for their families." Waightstill Avery visited "a poor Highlanders log Cabbin, measuring out 6 feet of ground." Not surprisingly, Avery slept outside that evening. Generally, the Highlanders lived in better houses in North Carolina than in Scotland, where they often lived in huts with no windows, and animals slept under the same roof. Some tacksmen, however, may have lowered their living standards when they first arrived. Even as individuals grew wealthier and their families expanded, they still continued to live in small quarters — perhaps with an additional room. Smyth, the English traveller, lodged with "a common plain back wood's planter" on the south bank of the Dan River. The man possessed "a large family of Bel Savages," who all lived in a one room house. The planter offered Smyth his bed, which Smyth politely turned down. Instead he slept "on a pallet spread on the floor from one side of the room to the other, on which every person of the family, excepting the Master and Mistress, lay promiscuously, men and women, boys and girls."[8]

Even a prosperous plantation did not imply a fine house, as Janet Schaw discovered. At Hunthill, John Rutherfurd's plantation, she found "a show of plenty ... beyond any thing I ever saw, but it is a mere plantation." She noted that Rutherfurd's dwelling was "little better than one of his Negro huts." And it particularly amused Miss Schaw "to eat out of China and be served in plate in such a parlour." In addition to this room, the house had a library well equipped with globes and mathematical instruments and a bed-room especially added for the expected guests. "Tho' the house is no house," Miss Schaw remarked, "yet the master and the furniture make you ample amends."[9] Hunthill was no exception, although it is surprising that Schaw did not mention an upper floor, unless it was merely a loft. The celebrated Orton mansion of the Moores and the Quinces, however, only had one floor in the colonial period. The cooking was obviously done in a separate build-ing, as was the case on most plantations.

The house of a planter or farmer who had obtained some degree of pros-perity was generally a two-story structure with two to four rooms on each floor plus a hall in the center. Simplicity governed its appearance both inside and outside. Walls might be plastered or on rare occasions fully paneled. Furniture was kept at a minimum. The homes of the wealthy were obviously comfortable, but also modest. The "Better Sort" apparently did not want to appear too arrogant. Mary Haynes wrote to her daughter that "it gives me pleasure to hear that ... you are so agreeably settled in your new house[.] I dare say you are not a little vane but remember to bless God that you have every thing that can render life desirable which those in the world are defsired [sic] of even those that have been born to affluence of fortune."[10]

The majority of North Carolinians (98 per cent) lived in the rural areas, and as a traveller pointed out, one could journey long distances without seeing more than one or two plantations. The family, which eighteenth-century clergymen referred to as the very basis of society, indeed, became the only community that many children knew in their early years; especially in the backcountry. One of the first reasons why James Iredell liked the Johnston family so much was the genuine affection that held the family together — both adults and children, siblings and cousins. Samuel Johnston clearly believed that as head of his family which included sisters, nephews, nieces, and cousins, he had certain specific responsibilities. But Johnston was certainly no exception. Other families apparently enjoyed the same warm relationship with each other. Given the sparse population and small houses, families undoubtedly became well-acquainted. Sons, when they grew old enough, worked alongside their fathers, while daughters learned housewifely tasks from their mothers. In fact, one reason that Tryon gave for there being few slaves in the Piedmont was the poverty of the settlers when they first arrived, and before they could "get into Sufficient affluence to buy Negroes their own Children" had "grown to an age to work in the Field."[11]

American parents supposedly indulged their children, and North Carolina parents (at least the wealthier) were no exception. The Reverend James Reed warned at least one schoolmaster about the "excessive Indulgence" of parents towards their children. But youngsters on the farm had to contribute their share of labor. Colonel William Few vividly recalled his arrival as a lad of ten in Orange County from Maryland. He then "commenced the occupation of farmer," and what better way in North Carolina than by cutting down a tree. In the beginning it was great fun, but "the business progressed very slowly," and he found his "situation most deplorable, for I dared not to resist the order I had received to cut down the tree." Nevertheless, he accomplished his task, and "was gradually instructed in the arts of agriculture; for that was all I had to learn. In that country, at that time, there were no schools." A year later, however, a schoolmaster came into the area and thus offered Few an escape from his chores.[12]

Children in more fortunate economic circumstances and in towns had more opportunity to be pampered. They had the time for games and races as well as the prospect of regular schooling. One German observer believed that English parents allowed their children to "grow up like domestic animals," without either baptism or schooling. English children did seem to manage more freedom than their German peers, but parents of either nationality realized the value of their offspring in a young country. Upon hearing of the birth of Samuel Johnston's first son, his English agent who had once lived in the colony offered his congratulations, an invitation to send the boy to England for his education and some advice on child care: "You must keep him out of the sun in summer and yet keep him out of Doors as much as possible, there is no other way of raising Children in your Climate."[13] The problems of child care and whether the child should be inside or outside did not cease with the Revolution. But what first concerned early American parents was the child's surviving infancy. Few families, regardless of their socioeconomic level, saw the survival of all their children to adulthood.

When the child was about seven years old, if circumstances allowed, he began to learn the three R's — at least to read the Bible, to write a rough scrawl, and to do arithmetic to the Rule of Three. If there were no schools or schoolmasters in the neighborhood, he waited as did William Few, for one to appear. The wealthier planters, instead of waiting for a schoolmaster to appear, would employ a tutor or would join some of his neighbors in hiring a schoolmaster. The local minister was often ready to prepare a few boys in the neighborhood for college as well. Or parents themselves might take over the pedagogy task.

Penelope Dawson, daughter of former Governor Gabriel Johnston, early a widow, had to manage the education of her children. She sent her son Billy to a neighborhood school in Bertie County, even though there was a free school in Edenton because she preferred Billy's not crossing the river. After the schoolmaster left the area, Mrs. Dawson herself supervised Billy's "reading four times a day & writing twice & I believe he was never kept half so strict with any of his masters." But she was happy that a new tutor was shortly expected to take over the school. Billy Dawson fortunately had a mother who could instruct him in the three R's when the schoolmaster decided to break up his school. Not all children were so fortunate.[14]

For most parents two years of schooling were deemed quite adequate. Hopefully the child had obtained some basic knowledge during that time. William Few had had two years of instruction, and those two years had been interrupted: six or eight months with a schoolmaster in Maryland and a year in North Carolina. The total expense for his education "did not exceed five dollars." The family, however, had helped to board the master and had "clothed [him] from the domestic loom." Few's lack of education did not stem from a lack of interest, although his Maryland master had been a very poor teacher, but from a lack of time and available schools. He continued to read and eventually became a lawyer. Not all young men who had had so little schooling did so well, but even Few did not question whether he should have had more formal instruction.[15]

Apprenticeship papers and guardian accounts give some idea of the minimum requirements demanded by the public. In 1755 the North Carolina legislature required orphans (both boys and girls) when they were apprenticed to be taught to read and write. In a survey of the Onslow County bonds during the Revolutionary Era, the county court ordered all children to be taught to read and write. The same was true of Rowan County in the West. Whether masters followed the court order is another matter, but the community, at least on paper, believed that all children should have some instruction in reading and writing. Of course, they also seemed to indicate that between one and two years was all the time required to obtain that training. In Edgecombe County in the years 1762 to 1778, the guardian accounts indicate that thirty-seven children received some instruction, but that instruction only averaged five months.[16]

The wealthier members of the community, however, like Mrs. Dawson, generally took more care of the education of their sons than simply being satisfied with a little knowledge in the three R's. Billy Dawson was finally sent to England. Other young men began their classical instruction by going to New Bern, Edenton, one of the Presbyterian academies in the West, or to Charles Town or one of the northern schools. After independence was gained, a number of academies were founded all over the state to provide a republican education. In grammar schools or academies, boys received training in the classics; that is, a "liberal education" that would prepare them for their role as gentlemen as well as for college or one of the professions. Such an education emphasized Latin and a little Greek, mathematics, rhetoric, logic, history, and philosophy — all subjects that were continued through the college years. For college instruction, of course, young men before 1793 had to go abroad or north for their higher degrees. Many went to Princeton, but at least two of the revolutionary leaders, Maurice Moore and Samuel Johnston, had gone to New England schools, where Governor Josiah Martin believed that they had imbibed democratic principles. Johnston's father and uncle both urged him to read Locke's *Essay on Human Understanding* while he was at Yale; no doubt he added Locke's *Treatise on Civil Government*.[17]

Wealthy families could afford to send their children elsewhere to school, but by the 1760s the "chief planters" had begun to see the necessity of establishing schools in the colony; a necessity that royal governors had seen for some time. Distances, geographic obstacles, and religious diversity, scarcity of both money and a large urban area all contributed to the lack of permanent schools. Before the 1760s, whether North Carolina could even have supported any free schools is highly questionable. The arrival of Thomas Thomlinson, an English schoolmaster, in New Bern in December, 1763, and his opening a school the following January provided the impetus for the assembly. In 1764 it passed an act to encourage the building of a schoolhouse in the capital, and two years later it incorporated a society to operate the school and provided a revenue for the education of ten poor children.[18]

The Reverend James Reed and Governor Tryon both praised Thomlinson as a scholar and "a man of good conduct." Tryon believed that the schoolmaster was "the only person of repute of that profession in the country." By 1767 the school's enrollment had peaked at eighty scholars, but it generally averaged sixty pupils who came from all over the province. In 1770 the school's enrollment had begun to decline because of the currency shortage and the expense of boarding children in New Bern. At the same time, a dissenting minister in Wilmington had opened up a school, so that six Cape Fear boys were withdrawn to attend classes closer to home. But what injured the school even more was Thomlinson's disciplining and expelling two unruly youngsters, the children of two trustees. Thomlinson had been careful about antagonizing parents and disciplining children but finally had had to assert his authority, which brought about his dismissal — much to the detriment of the school.[19]

In 1770 the assembly also incorporated the Edenton Free School. Both the governor and the assembly would like to have provided for an academy in the West as well, but only Presbyterian grammar schools were found there. In 1771 the assembly passed a bill to found Queen's Museum in Charlotte and referred to "several Grammar schools [that] have been long taught in the western parts of this Government, in which many students have very considerable progress in the languages and other literary attainments." The assembly decided that one of the schools should have a lasting foundation and should be made a college. The crown disallowed the act because the school was Presbyterian. It continued to operate as Liberty Hall Academy. Only after the colony had become a state could dissenting schools secure legal recognition.[20]

Some North Carolina children, then, received an education, but that generalization, however accurate, does not mean that any child who wanted an education could have it, or that there were plenty of schools, or that the quality was high. According to letters written in the first decade of the nineteenth century, educational opportunities before and during the War for Independence were extremely limited. A resident of Caswell County believed that before 1776 "not more than one third of the inhabitants could read, and scarcely half that number could write a legible hand: from 1775 to 1800 what was then called a common english education, viz. 'to read, write, and cypher as far as the rule of three' was given to a little more than half the inhabitants." Another writer was more pessimistic in his figures since he believed that one-third of the adult residents in Edgecombe County could not read in 1811 — which was an improvement over the Revolutionary Era. He believed that only one-third of the women then living in Edgecombe could write which, of course, points out another facet in the educational process.[21]

A liberal education, whether it was secured through private or public means, belonged to the male world. Young ladies had to be satisfied with the "Feminine Accomplishments." And in North Carolina, where there were no boarding schools or few travelling music masters, young ladies were seemingly destitute of acquiring a proper instruction. English schools were normally open to both sexes, and farmers' daughters often learned the three R's in the same classroom as their brothers. But there their formal education stopped unless they pursued it under their mothers or a governess, or music and French masters who happened to be in the neighborhood, or unless they were sent to a boarding school in Charles Town or one of the northern cities. Only daughters of wealthy planters could hope for such luxury. Even then many fathers who could afford it hated to send their little girls — a more fragile commodity than their sons — abroad for additional training.

What should a little girl learn? How to pick a husband would be the answer given by the *North Carolina Magazine* in 1764:

'Tis question whether one in ten
Knows how to spell her name; — what then!
She's been three years, or more at school,
And learn'd to compliment by rule;
Learn'd how to dress, and how to dance;
Can tell what mode came last from France;
Can cut a fowl the modish way,
And knows the art of drinking tea.
On these acquirements, when compounded,
Is female education grounded.[22]

The poem then proceeds to tell young ladies to be aware of certain types such as fops or rakes. Although satiric, the verse contained much truth about the education of young ladies — whether in North Carolina, another colony, or in England. The results of such an education (or of catching such a husband) can partially be seen in the smitten Iredell's description of Hannah Johnston:

Her understanding is uncommonly excellent, and it has been improved by much useful and elegant reading.... Her conversation ... such as you would suppose for a young lady whose mind is disposed to every good and benevolent action. ... She perfectly understands the use of her needle, and is a professed enemy to the feminine weakness of attachment to fine clothes and gaudy appearance ... [she] always ... wear[s] a dress of decency, neatness and propriety.[23]

To be able to read and discuss (at least superficially) literature, such as the *Spectator* and some history, to speak well, to write a "pretty hand," to know a little geography, to play musical instruments, to do fancy needlework — all these attributes (the goals of feminine education) formed the proper lady, and once these attainments were acquired, finding a proper husband should be easy.

Daughters of middling folk, of course, did not have to worry about the "Feminine Accomplishments" as such. But they still needed to learn the housewifely tasks and to act with modesty and propriety. Observers, however, doubted that backcountry girls learned much modesty as long as they dressed and slept in the same room as the male members of their families and wore only shifts on hot summer days.

On the whole, North Carolina mothers must have done an admirable job of raising their daughters. Janet Schaw, critical of American men, especially praised American women. She was amazed at the difference between the two sexes, but "a sensible man" who had lived in the colony for some time believed that it was due to the manner in which girls had been reared. "In the infancy of this province, said he, many families from Britain came over, and of these the wives and daughters were people of education." The mothers instructed their daughters "in the family duties necessary to the sex" and "in those accomplishments and genteel manners that are still so visible amongst them, and this descended from Mother to daughter." The father took his son to the woods "and taught the sturdy lad to glory in the stroke he could give with his Ax, in the trees he felled, and the deer he shot." Through this process young men "lost every art or science," and even after they were no longer required to carve their homes out of the wilderness, still found it necessary "to spend their time abroad in the fields; and to be a good marksman." Men, of course, had more education to lose in the first place.[24]

Francisco de Miranda, the Spanish adventurer, loved the North Carolina ladies (both figuratively and literally) and noted that their manner was "somewhat reserved, but when one has gained their friendship and is well known to them, they are both agreeable and charming." Miranda found the married ones, however, a bit too reserved. They "observe a monastic seclusion, and such submission to their husbands as I have never seen." He described their lifestyle as totally "domestic." "As soon as they marry they separate themselves from all intimate friendships, and their attentions are centered entirely upon the care of their house and family; the first year as married women they spend in the role of lovers, the second as nursemaids, and the third and remaining years as housekeepers. The spinsters, on the other hand, enjoy complete liberty, and go walking alone wherever they please, without their steps being watched."[25]

Miranda, whether he fully realized it or not, observed the paradox in the education of young ladies in the Anglo-American world. Before marriage young ladies could play the coquette, could enjoy the degree of worldliness (yet they always had to be discreet in being the flirt), but after marriage they had no choice but to become the nursemaid and housewife. In fact, any freedom of choice for the young lady ended at courtship.

When the young man decided that his circumstances permitted, he could begin to think about settling down. The manner by which one courted and proposed marriage depended on one's status. For John and Molly in the Piedmont, the decision might be theirs alone, and they immediately set up housekeeping. But for James Iredell and Hannah Johnston, the process meant one of formally asking her guardian, her brother, for permission — even though they had decided to marry, and Hannah was twenty-six years old. Not all marriages were love-matches, however, and not all love-matches were sanctioned. James Iredell shortly before his marriage noted in his journal that he had heard that Nancy Rainbough, who was marrying the innkeeper Horniblow, "was averse to the match, forced to it by her father and mother." He wondered if it were true. Could "such parents exist? and a too easy, too compliant daughter with the desires of parents, in a point they have no right to *command.*" Iredell, who had just finished reading *Clarissa Harlowe,* had not learned Samuel Richardson's lesson that daughters should obey their parents in such circumstances.[26]

Whether many parents forced their wishes upon their daughters is left to the realm of speculation, since social institutions were not yet firmly fixed in the colony. Mary Burgwyn, gossiping to her sister, reported that Miss Mosley (daughter of an aristocratic family) was going to marry "one Monroe," the illegitimate son of a Captain Monroe. "The Match is entirely disagreeable to all her friends. Her mother has even been on her Knees to her without effect." Penelope Johnston Dawson, sent to Williamsburg to meet the best people, met John Dawson, son of Virginia's commissary. Because her guardian disapproved, they eloped. James Murray did not want his niece to marry the "imprudent" William Hooper (a radical), but love nevertheless prevailed.[27]

A German pastor warned his young men about marrying English or Irish girls. He found that "the Irish in this section are lazy, dissipated and poor, live in the most wretched huts and enjoy the same food as their animals (although in the cities this matter is reversed)." Irish girls clearly would be poor housewives, but on the other hand it was "very seldom that German and English blood is happily united in wedlock. Dissentions and feeble Children are often the result." Nor would the English wife "permit her husband to be master in his household, and when he likewise insists upon his rights Crime and murder ensue." Whether the pastor literally meant that murder would occur, he left vague, but once married one did find it difficult to escape, unless one "eloped," which occasionally happened. Since the Anglican church was established in North Carolina, divorces were difficult to obtain. There were no ecclesiastical courts, so one had to go to the legislature. Sometimes a legal separation was approved. One of the revolutionary heroes, Robert Howe, for instance, was legally separated from his wife. Men could always escape the confines of marriage by keeping a mistress or by visiting the slave quarters. A Jamaican merchant, however, reported that in North Carolina he "found an empty House, the late Tenant of which had been oblig'd by the Church Wardens to decamp on Account of his having kept a Black Woman. Dont suppose Fornication is out of Fashion here ... more than in other Places, No! the difference only is, that the White Girls monopolize it."[28]

The house and the dairy were the woman's domain. While her husband was busy plowing the fields or marketing the crops, the mistress of the plantation or farm was cleaning, cooking, washing, managing the dairy, tending the garden, and caring for the children. If the family owned slaves, she might not be as involved in some of the manual labor, but she was still supervising the same tasks, and household servants were evidently not as numerous in the colony as in either Virginia or South Carolina. Miss Schaw found her sister-in-law "a most excellent wife and a fond mother. Her dairy and her garden show her industry, tho' even there she is an American." The Scottish lady believed that her brother had "no cause to complain"; that his wife was not only agreeable, but "if she would pay" her personal appearance "a little more attention, it would be lovely." Miss Schaw also praised another American woman, the wife of Cornelius Harnett, "Wilmington's Sam Adams," for her activities as a gardener and housewife although she never had the opportunity of meeting the lady. Mary Harnett, according to Schaw, supplied Wilmington "with what vegetables they use, also with mellons and other fruits. She even descends to make minced pies, cheese-cakes, tarts and little biskets, which she sends down to town once or twice a day, besides her eggs, poultry and butter, and she is the only one who continues to have Milk." Either Wilmington residents did not require many vegetables because they had their own gardens or Mrs. Harnett had an extremely productive garden. The Harnetts certainly did not need the money, but perhaps Mrs. Harnett was finding an emotional outlet — because she did not have children and had good business sense — or perhaps it was because her husband was such a "brute," as Janet Schaw believed.[29]

For some women, home, garden, and dairy were not their only concern. Because of the death of their husbands, they found themselves managing plantations, ferries, ordinaries, or shops. Penelope Dawson, although with the advice of her cousin Samuel Johnston and her overseer, still managed her various lands; from settling labor-management problems to the purchase of supplies to planting matters. At one point, however, she asked Johnston to write the overseer because she believed that he "would have a much better effect than my doing it." She obviously recognized that a plantation overseer would listen more carefully to a man than a woman. Mrs. Cobb, the eighty-three year old innkeeper, continued her operations because she prided "herself on her activity, and attention to her Guests and to their Horses." Attmore found her "as brisk and lively as most Women of 30 years of Age" and that she herself took care of the horses and brought in the wood for the fire. Elizabeth Gillespie in Salisbury lost her husband in 1759; in 1760 she purchased a lot on which she built and operated an inn. She continued to buy pieces of land, which led one historian to write that "the extent and location of her purchases indicates that she was a shrewd, capable woman." Even after her marriage she and her husband continued her various business ventures. The widows of merchants also continued to operate shops; for example, Mrs. Edward Batchelor and Jean Blair.[30]

Women served as executors of estates, could inherit land and take out land grants. Although they could not become directly involved in politics, they took an active interest. The young ladies of Mecklenburg and Rowan counties made their own declaration in 1776: to be courted only by young gentlemen who did their military duty. And the Edenton ladies held their famous tea party. But more important during the war were the activities on the home front. Elkanah Watson, after Independence, witnessed a very obese lady at Warrenton who appeared to be a leader at the polls. He thought that it was very humorous and pointed her out to his host, Colonel Hill. When he went to dinner that evening he once again saw the woman who was the colonel's mother. Watson "was soon relieved from my awkward position, by her kindness and affability. ... I never met with a more sensible, spirited old lady. She was a great politician; and I was assured that she had more political influence, and exerted it with greater effect, than any man in her county."[31]

One activity that took women out of the house was the visiting of relatives and friends. Although North Carolinians had not developed the art of visiting as highly as their Virginia neighbors, they were headed in that direction. That they loved company and opened their doors to strangers has already been noted. Wealthy planters also exchanged visits with each other. One of the seats of hospitality in the Albemarle region was Eden Hall, the home of Penelope Dawson. She, and her husband while he was still living, regularly entertained guests, not only including relatives but also neighbors and friends. For the amusement of one Presbyterian gentleman, Mr. Dawson sent for a drunken parson.[32]

Merchants and lawyers were often on the road and sometimes their wives accompanied them for a holiday, although it was not the normal practice since wives usually stayed at home to take care of the children. On one occasion Johnston and Iredell, while riding the circuit, stopped to have breakfast with the newlywed Richard Bennehans, who operated the Snow Camp store in Orange County. The two lawyers had intended to stay only a short time, but at Bennehan's insistence, they stayed the whole day. William Johnston, Bennehan's partner, was sent for "and we had a happy day in company with them and Mrs. Bennyam, whose amiableness of temper is extremely engaging," but Iredell believed that her life must be very dull. "She has not a single woman she can associate with nearer than Hillsborough, which is at the distance of 18 miles." When Johnston "told her he would endeavor to bring Mrs. Johnston to see her, she could scarcely speak; tears flowed into her eyes."[33] A sparse population and distant neighbors easily made visiting the most popular form of entertainment for many Carolinians.

Besides visiting, Carolinians especially enjoyed having balls in the towns — or striking up a fiddle and having some dancing in the country — and attending theatrical performances whenever a company or an entertainer happened to pass through the area. Gentlemen occasionally played backgammon; and billiards were popular in both Wilmington and Edenton. But, perhaps, horses and horse races were as popular as any form of sport. Attmore mentioned the extreme excitement over a horse race and the spirited betting that took place among all segments of the population. The existent newspapers often advertised good breeding horses, and Cosmos (one of the more famous) had been heard of by the British army. Samuel Johnston wrote his sister from Halifax at the beginning of the war that horses instead of politics were the general topic of conversation. Only "Gen. Lee and his dogs had entirely supplanted the horses." Among the stories that Halifax residents were telling at the time was one on themselves: "the general will not suffer Spado to eat bacon for breakfast (a practice very general both with gentlemen and ladies in this part of the country) lest it should make him stupid." The residents of Halifax, despite the general's remarks, still liked Lee.[34]

According to travellers, North Carolinians found plenty of time for leisure; even those "enervated by age or infirmity" who always had the "consolation" of "drinking grog." And holidays were always welcomed — by both whites and blacks. But one German visitor believed that neither race needed the rest. "It is difficult to say which are the best creatures, the whites here or their blacks, or which have been formed by the others; but in either case their example is bad. The white men are all the time complaining that the blacks will not work and they themselves do nothing." The same observer, however, later talked about the work demanded by slaves in more sympathetic terms and was especially touched by an auction at Wilmington. He witnessed the sale of "a cooper, indispensible in pitch and tar making, [who] cost his purchaser 250 Pd., and his 15-year old boy, bred to the same work, [who] fetched 150 Pd. The father was put up first; his anxiety lest his son fall to another purchaser and be separated from him was more painful than his fear of getting into the hands of a hard master." Fortunately for the two, they became the property of the same owner. Not all slave families were so lucky.[35]

Janet Schaw also respected the labor done by slaves and believed that Negroes, with respect to their gardens and animals, were more industrious than the poor whites. She believed that they were "the only people that seem to pay any attention to the various uses that the wild vegetables may be put to," and that they cultivated their gardens "much better than their Master." They also raised "hogs and poultry, sow calabrashes, etc. and are better provided for in every thing than the poorer white people with us." On the other hand, she noted that "they steal what ever they can come at, and even intercept the cows and milk them. They are indeed the constant plague of their tyrants."[36] The "constant plague" or not, for men like John Rutherfurd on whose plantation Miss Schaw saw slaves working at the sawmills and producing naval stores, they made up an extremely efficient labor force. In fact, in the large-scale production of naval stores and lumber, slaves almost exclusively made up the labor force.

Slavery was not as important, however, an institution in North Carolina as in the neighboring colonies. But legally it was just as firmly established as in South Carolina and in the beginning of settlement (since the Carolinas were then one colony) had shared the same slave code. North Carolinians also shared the same attitudes toward Negroes; and the institution, though on a smaller scale, was just as cruel and oppressive. The fact that there were smaller numbers of slaves, that there were no absentee landlords, that holdings were small, for the most part, contributed to a paternalism often found later on farms and plantations in the Upper South. Scotus Americanus told the Highlanders that once they had the money, they should invest it in slaves, and the writer boasted that blacks were treated better in Carolina than on the Sugar Islands. "Good usage is what alone can make the negroes well attached to their masters interest."[37] The paternalism shown toward slaves, though destructive of the slaves' manhood, also underscored a measure of humanity.

Letters of Penelope Dawson and Samuel Johnston show the personal contact between slaves and their masters — with the overseer sometimes in the role of the villain. At one point, one of Mrs. Dawson's slaves came to her "with a grievous complaint of being starved, & that he was sure the Negroes would all leave the plantation if there was not an alternation made." Mrs. Dawson — "thinking that you be able to judge better from seeing him yourself" — decided to send the slave to Johnston. She believed that there might be some truth to the story since corn was scarce and the slaves were living "much harder than ever they did before" and the overseer might be "too saving of the Wheat." In another letter Mrs. Dawson informed Johnston that Callum might "plague" him because "he would not rest till I promised to let you know that one of the girls that are hired out is his wife, & entreats very hard that she may be suffered to stay on the plantation. I never met with such a pleader, I told him I did not imagine it would be to any purpose to trouble you about it but he insisted upon it that if you knew she was his wife you would let her stay, as it would prevent his ever running about from the plantation so that he seem to think himself a person of the utmost consequence."[38]

A traveller going through the southern colonies believed that owners with "the largest droves" kept their slaves in the worst condition, "let them run

Slave Cabin

naked mostly or in rags, and accustom them as much as possible to hunger, but exact of them steady work." But the slaves in the Dawson-Johnston holdings apparently were as satisfied as any who belonged to a smaller slaveowner. Johnston, indeed, purchased from the estate of a loyalist friend, Nathaniel Duckenfield, "three of the old Negroes besides Toney who importuned me with tears streaming from their Eyes not to let them fall into the hands of strangers." They emphasized that "they were worn out with labour." Their entreaties, plus those of Johnston's sister, "prevailed on me to purchase them, tho they are ... almost altogether useless by their age & infirmities." Mrs. Dawson also purchased one "who begged that he might not be parted from his Wife & Children." In a letter from Duckenfield to Johnston, the Englishman sent a message to Toney that the latter's son Andrew had a position with an officer of the guard and that the last time Duckenfield had seen Andrew, he had wanted to establish an "Eating House." The Duckenfield slaves had managed to exploit the paternalistic feelings of their master's friends for some stability in their own lives.[39]

Dr. Bray's Associates, an English philanthropic organization, interested in the religious instruction of Negroes, investigated the possibility of educating young blacks in North Carolina in the 1760s. In doing so, the Associates discovered the prejudices of white Carolinians as well as the difficulty of establishing schools — whether for white or black children. The Reverend Mr. Alexander Stewart of Bath explained some of these difficulties: first, the location of the coastal towns, "where Negroes are most to be had ... on very Wide Rivers, often Impracticable to Cross," which cut "off one half of the Country Children"; second, the expense, then, "of boarding negroe Children"; third, the "loss of their time"; and finally, "the Prejudices of the Ignorant." Nevertheless, one of the schoolmasters in Stewart's parish was willing to instruct black children, even though there were few masters who had "the Salvation of Negroes Souls at heart." Six months later Stewart reported that as long as he only discussed the project of schools for Negro children, "he was fed with Hopes," but once he had actually started distributing books, and the schoolmasters had begun teaching, Stewart found "that it was but Labour & Sorrow owing to the mean low Prejudices of the People."[40]

Dr. Bray's Associates also tried to establish a school in the Cape Fear region — either at Wilmington or Brunswick. Since there was no minister, they sent books to Lewis DeRossett (a Cape Fear merchant and member of the governor's council) who thought that a schoolmaster or mistress might be found to teach both white and black children; but DeRossett found that Wilmington residents did not want "their Children Associating with Slaves." He indicated that the prejudices of the local people were "deeply rooted." Two years later, the new rector at Brunswick tried a different approach. He thought that by having a schoolmistress teach black girls sewing, knitting, and marking, the people would want "to send young

Negroe girls," but instead he found that slaveowners "would rather their Slaves wou'd remain Ignorant as brutes." In Albemarle, the Reverend Daniel Earl also noted that black and white children could not be taught in the same room. Since only "the affluent" would send their Negro children, Mr. Earle believed that it was not worth the endeavor. He then asked for support for the schooling of white children.[41]

It is unlikely that many slaves received any sort of religious instruction during the Revolutionary period. There were few missionaries in the colony, and they had their hands full with their white parishioners. Owners apparently had little desire for their slaves to be Christianized. James Reed believed that most Negroes were heathen. But one of his colleagues mentioned that near Brunswick there were numerous New Light Baptists who allowed "even Negroes [to speak] in their meetings." Evidently not all prejudices were firmly rooted. And some blacks also obtained a little education. One runaway was described as a "sensible Fellow, and slow of Speech; he can read, write, and cypher." That the Negro was both a runaway and a literate individual must have indicated to some masters that a little education could be harmful.[42]

North Carolinians feared a slave revolt; a fear that is constantly present in a society that maintains slavery. The Act of 1741 concerning servants and slaves, passed after the Stono Rebellion in South Carolina and a revision of an earlier act, formed the basis of the colony's slave code; a code that was designed to maintain order and to prevent the possibility of insurrection. The law only allowed one slave on a plantation to possess a gun for hunting and provided various punishments for runaway Negroes and for destruction of property. Local communities also passed specific regulations. Wilmington would not allow slaves to maintain separate residences, engage in business transactions "without having a Ticket from the Master, Mistress [or] Overseer." It forbade the "playing, Riotting, or Caballing" together of four or more slaves and declared a ten o'clock curfew. It also fined individuals who sold rum to Negroes. There was no major insurrection in colonial North Carolina, but the fear was still there. On the eve of the War for Independence rumors spread that Governor Martin had promised blacks their freedom if they would fight against the whites. The rumor proved false, but Janet Schaw found that in Wilmington it had brought tories and whigs together against the common threat. Although there were no violent outbursts, slaves did manage to resist the institution in various ways: by destruction of property, theft, drinking, and running away.[43]

The Revolution did not change the status of slaves although the slave code by the end of the eighteenth century guaranteed them some basic rights; primarily the right of life. Killing a Negro became a homicide in 1774 for the first time. Slavery grew in the last two decades of the eighteenth century as more farmers could afford slaves and as cotton became important. A Pennsylvanian reported an argument at dinner between two gentlemen over the question of slavery. Judge Samuel Spencer "wished that there was an immediate addition of One Hundred Thousand Slaves to the State." He "frankly declared that his views were for the present ease and affluence," even though later generations might suffer.[44] The judge freely admitted what many whites probably found it very hard to do. Only the Quakers were openly engaged in any antislavery activities before 1790.

That slaveholders should scarcely care about the salvation of their slaves should have come as no surprise to pious laymen and Anglican ministers when the latter often complained about the immoralities and ignorance of white parishioners. Throughout the eighteenth century until the War for Independence, Anglican missionaries when they were present in the colony railed against the improprieties — the slothfulness, ignorance, and heathenish attitudes of North Carolinians. The Reverend Mr. John MacDowell, while complaining about his salary, defined the character of St. Philip's (Brunswick) vestry in the following manner: "one of them declared that the money he is obliged to give to the maintaining a minister, he would rather give to a kind girl. Another is a person who committed incest, with his own uncles widow & has a child by her which he owns publicly — another believes there is neither Hell nor Devil." A year earlier MacDowell had commented that a lot of good could be accomplished in North Carolina, "a Country inhabited by many sorts of People, of various nations and different opinions, customs and manners." But more and more MacDowell became concerned about his own well-being and preservation.[45]

North Carolina presented clergymen with a challenge. From the letters sent to England, she appeared a religious frontier, where the dregs of society lived — an assignment that nobody would want or could tolerate — that only the most dedicated or adventurous would consider. In reality, the Church of England, though established, was confronted by aggressive, enthusiastic sects on the one hand, often Deistic vestries on the other, and a slew of unchurched people in the middle. The Bishop of London granted licenses to over 700 clergymen to serve in the American colonies; but of that number, only forty-four were appointed to North Carolina, and not all of them made it. In 1764 Governor Arthur Dobbs reported six resident clergymen, "four of which are pious, & perform their duty, the other two very indifferent & of suspicious morals." Tryon as soon as he came into office attempted to deal with one of the latter, an itinerant missionary who was licensed to preach "everywhere," but "seldom preaches any where." Unfortunately for the church, not all its representatives were men of the highest caliber. The Reverend C. E. Taylor described his predecessor as having "fled into Virginia, being charged with crimes, too base to be mentioned." He also did not think much of the Reverend Daniel Earl of Edenton who frequented public houses and was more engaged in fishing for herring than for lost souls.[46]

After Tryon became governor, he attempted to strengthen the church establishment by securing its finances, by pushing for the right of presentment (the governor's right, in the absence of a bishop, to install a clergyman in a parish), by obtaining more appointments, and by watching for any deviance among the clergy. Presentment posed the biggest problem. The governor managed to present a few clergymen, but several vestries balked. And rectors in those parishes did not push to be presented. They realized that their vestries had no intention of giving up any power that they had gained by the absence of a bishop. By the end of Tryon's administration, however, eighteen parishes did have rectors. The Church of England, then, saw its most rapid expansion in the Revolutionary Era. Just as it was finally becoming a viable force, however, independence removed government support and discredited a number of Anglican ministers. In the 1780s, it was struggling to survive.

Whether a majority of North Carolinians were Anglican in the colonial period is only probable. Because of the settlement of various ethnic groups with strong religious ties, a number of residents belonged to dissenting congregations. In 1765 Tryon believed that the majority of North Carolinians belonged to the Church of England; even so, "every sect of religion abounds here except the Roman Catholic and by the best information I can get Presbytery and a sect who called themselves New Lights (not of the flock of Mr. Whitefield) but Superior Lights from New England, appear in the front." Four years later Tryon believed that establishing "the preeminence" of the Church of England had caused the other denominations to be jealous, but he still stated that it was not religion but scarcity of money that made "many parishes very slack to encourage public worship." At the same time he wrote that "the Presbyterians and Quakers are the only tolerated sectaries under any order or regulation, every other are enemies to society and a scandal to common sense."[47] Tryon especially gave preferential treatment to the Presbyterians, who could be married by their own clergymen. And they responded to their privileged position by staying out of the regulator movement. Perhaps as a reward for that action, Tryon approved the projected founding of Queen's Museum (not to be confused with the Queen's College now located in Charlotte), although the crown later disallowed the act.

In those parishes where the majority of people were not Anglican, the electors simply voted for a vestry that would not qualify. One Anglican minister appointed to Mecklenburg County decided to go to another parish after he was told how "uneasy" his life would be if he attempted to hold services there. The majority of residents in Mecklenburg were clearly Presbyterian and would not elect a supportive vestry. In Rowan where there were also many Presbyterians as well as German Reform and Lutheran, the Reverend Theodorus Swaine Draige attempted to fill St. Luke's parish. He believed that the majority of people were Anglican, but he had difficulty in getting an Anglican vestry elected. He became embroiled in local politics and finally went to South Carolina in despair. Earlier he had written Tryon

St. John's Episcopal Church, originally built 1771-1773, has been restored in Williamsborough in Vance County.

69

that the dissenters say that they "have a right to oppose any intrusion on their religious rights, a Maxim I presume dangerous in itself [not only] with respect to this county and the neighboring counties, but the whole Back Frontier of America."[48]

There were problems in eastern parishes as well. Even if a clergyman had a duly constituted vestry governing the parish, he might have to wait for his salary because of a delinquent sheriff. In a county where Presbyterians dominated, even if a vestry did not qualify, care for the poor would still be provided. But the assembly had to pass a special act to take care of the poor in Pasquotank County where no vestry would qualify. There were large numbers of Baptists (and some notable Baptist leaders) in that county, which probably explained the lack of parish government. Tryon had called St. Johns, Pasquotank, a weak parish with reference to its ability to support a minister, but perhaps he also had the Baptist influence in mind.[49]

The religious pattern of the colony followed closely the settlement of ethnic groups. In the upper Cape Fear, Anson and Cumberland counties, where the Scottish Highlanders settled, Presbyterianism predominated. It was strengthened by the settlement of Scotch-Irish who extended into Rowan and Mecklenburg counties. Germans primarily settled in Rowan County and brought with them Lutheranism or Calvinism (Reform) and their own teachers. No churches, however, were actually organized until the 1770s. The most prominent group of Germans, of course, were the Moravians, who settled the Wachovia tract (originally in Rowan). The Moravians were recognized as a distinct parish within the Church of England's jurisdiction.

The older settlers in the coastal area and northern tier of counties had come primarily from an English background via England or South Carolina or Virginia. The majority had been christened in the Church of England, although there were a few English Baptists. In the Albemarle many older residents had been or were Quakers. By mid-century Quakers had also moved into the interior or had migrated from Pennsylvania or Virginia into the Piedmont. In the West, the Quakers first settled near Snow Camp. From there they expanded south and west.

Into the religious maze in the Piedmont came the Baptists. They did not make their gains with other dissenting groups, but with English settlers and adherents to the Church of England. As one Baptist historian points out, they were the only ones left that could be reached:

The Scotch Highlanders in Cumberland and the Germans in Randolph and Guilford and along the Yadkin could understand only those who used their own tongues. The Quakers of Cane Creek and New Garden were so well established in the tenets of their own faith that their conversion to another was not to be expected. The Moravians were a closely organized church and well satisfied with their beliefs. The Presbyterians who extended in a ring around the northern and western parts of the settlements had all the conservatism that has always characterized members of the Church of Scotland; they were served occasionally by able ministers, and were open to missionary influence by apostles of other faiths only when left too long without a visit from Presbyterian ministers.[50]

On the other hand, the English inhabitants in the West had no churches or ministers until after 1765, and they furnished a fertile field for missionary work.

In 1755 Shubal Stearns, the Baptist revivalist, and his family had arrived in the Sandy Creek settlement (at the time Orange County) and in a short time they built up their church congregation from sixteen members to 606. Revivalists (Separate Baptists) went out from Sandy Creek and converted numbers of individuals, and meeting houses were rapidly built. The doctrine of rebirth and the emphasis on a personal relationship with God attracted individuals who had had little contact with religion, but even more appealing was the manner by which Stearns and his followers preached. They utilized the "new preaching" that came out of the Great Awakening. Stearns's voice was described as "musical and strong." A particularly persuasive speaker, he could begin his preaching by making "soft impressions on the heart, and fetch tears from the eye in a mechanical way," and could then almost immediately change his manner "to shake the nerves, and to throw the animal system into tumults and perturbations." Women also spoke, and Stearns's sister, described as "a lady of good sense, singular piety, and surprising elocution," frequently "melted a whole concourse into tears by her prayers and exhortations."[51]

Baptists had lived in the East throughout the eighteenth century, but not until the Separate Baptists came did the establishment have real cause for alarm. Nearly the whole population of Onslow (which Parson Alexander Stewart described as "the present seat of enthusiasm") became Baptist, and there were strong Baptist meetings in the Albemarle region. Ezekiel Hunter, a Baptist minister, served in the General Assembly from Onslow; and after the War for Independence began, Pasquotank often included prominent Baptists in its legislative delegation. Henry Abbot, a Baptist minister from Pasquotank, introduced the resolution to the Halifax Congress in 1776 that all Protestant ministers should be able to perform the marriage ceremony.[52] The Anglican establishment had reason to fear the volatile Baptists of the 1760s who were more actively opposed to an established church than the older Baptist settlers had been. Many of the Separates after the regulator movement migrated to Tennessee or to the Georgia and South Carolina frontiers, but enough remained to continue to antagonize the establishment.

The New Light presence in the 1760s and 1770s could not be ignored — no doubt one of the reasons that Tryon wished to secure the establishment. Besides complaining, some Anglican ministers attempted to halt the influence by using similar tactics. The Reverend Mr. Stewart sometimes baptized by immersion to keep his parishioners in the fold. The Reverend Mr. Reed invited George Whitefield to preach in Christ Church. The Reverend Mr. Taylor believed that the Baptists were decreasing in Northampton County in the early 1770s due to his efforts, but in 1774 he began having trouble with "sectarists" from many different denominations, who "pretend to a familiar intercourse with the Son of God." He especially criticized the Reverend Mr. Devereux Jarratt who sometimes travelled into Carolina from his Virginia parish and "laid aside the service of the church" and used "extempore prayers and discourses" on free grace.[53] Regardless of their efforts, the Anglican clergy could not stem the impact of Great Awakening doctrines and methods of preaching in the colony. Even some of their own were using those methods. The people's acceptance of the doctrines of rebirth and the emphasis on the individual appealed to the inherent individualism of most North Carolinians as well as their lack of earlier religious experience. They eagerly responded to the call for a spiritual reawakening, and a one-to-one relationship with God.

The War for Independence discredited the Church of England because it represented a tie to England and had received the support of the royal government; many of its ministers were loyalists or men with loyalist inclinations. Only five Episcopal ministers lived in the state at the close of the war. The Quakers and Moravians, because of their pacifist beliefs, were regarded with suspicion by their neighbors. In contrast, the Presbyterians and Baptists (including their ministers) had strong ties with the patriot side, and in the making of the new state constitution they made certain that there would be a separation of church and state; that no denomination would receive a privileged position. Only Catholics and Jews were barred from political activity.

North Carolinians had their detractors in the eighteenth century. But much of that criticism stemmed from the lack of a structured social order, which stemmed in part from the colony's still being very much a frontier, even in the late eighteenth century — where social institutions were only beginning to gain stability and where society was extremely mobile and included a number of self-made men. Recent apologists have tried to show that North Carolinians were literate, that they were religious, that they were industrious, that they even included within their number a genteel group of planters. And there were people living in the colony who fitted all those categories. But there were a number of people who could not read or write (or at most could only sign their names) because they did not have the opportunity. There were a number of people who had no contact with any church which may have contributed to an irreligious feeling on the one hand, or a thirst for religion on the other, as is demonstrated by the Baptist successes. But either situation should not detract from the successful attempts of these people to build a home in a fertile and lush new land. Many Carolinians did not have the leisure time to enjoy the amenities of life. Nor had the wealthy had an opportunity to display lavishly their wealth. Many families were isolated, which strengthened provincial attitudes. Individualism characterized North Carolinians in their essentially middle-class culture; but one which acknowledged class lines. Although individualistic, their lifestyles were remarkably similar as well as their values. They lived comfortably; yet they hoped to improve their status. They represented a group of people that were not wholly unified, who were more closely tied to their local communities than their central government, but who were attempting to become a civilized society.

EPILOGUE

The War for Independence could not help but disrupt North Carolina society. The new state government had to enlist men in the military effort, requisition supplies for the army, find ways by which to finance the war, cope with fluctuating prices and a depreciating currency. Merchants had to change their trade patterns, and some of the less reputable became involved in wartime racketeering. Certain commodities became scarce as ports once open closed to American ships. To find goods such as sugar became a challenge for the housewife. Farming continued, but many men, including young boys, joined the army. Schools disbanded. From 1778 to 1783 North Carolina went without any kind of newspaper. The Church of England was thoroughly demoralized. Friendships had either been destroyed or had at least been made tenuous as a result of divided loyalties. But once the fighting had stopped, and North Carolinians had again settled down to peacetime endeavors, their society appeared much as it had before the war.

The majority of people still lived in rural areas and cultivated the soil for their living. Farmers continued to grow the same crops, except tobacco production in the 1780s greatly increased and naval stores shipments somewhat decreased because the bounty from the British was no longer in effect. The new state now exported its products primarily to other American ports or to the West Indies; only 10 per cent of North Carolina's trade was conducted with Great Britain. Scarcity of money, a difficulty before 1776, became an even greater problem in the 1780s (as in most of the new states). Specie disappeared; paper currency became worthless, which not only strained the economy but increased the tensions between debtors and creditors. Merchants especially aroused antagonism in the 1780s, as their values seemed to subvert the traditional values of North Carolina's agrarian society — at least, as far as many farmers were concerned. "What a Sett of Atheistical fellows," wrote an Orange County planter, Thomas Hart, in 1780 about New Bern's merchants, who think that"there is Neither God nor Devil to punish them in a Nother World, for their usury to us [the tobacco farmers] in this." Hart threatened to send Hawfield's Presbyterian minister, the Reverend Mr. John Debow "once more to preach up the Doctrine of Regeneration or the New Birth" because, he believed, there was never a "Sett of men on the face of this Globe, who stood more in Need of being Regenerated and Born anew," than the New Bern merchants.[1]

Aside from the problem of finance, North Carolinians also faced the problem of relocating the capital to a more central part of the state. One could not pinpoint the location of the central government in the 1780s, just as before 1765, when the colony had had no capital. Various towns competed for the honor of hosting the legislature, while public officials conducted business from their homes. When William Attmore visited North Carolina in 1787, the legislature was meeting at Tarborough, which had a population of about twenty families, and yet it successfully accommodated 120 assemblymen and sixty senators plus a number of persons (especially lawyers and merchants) interested in the legislative proceedings. North Carolina, thus, still had many decentralizing elements in its midst and continued to be very provincial. The people, many of them still isolated as the population pushed westward, were not unified. Yet the state had drafted one of the most radical of the new state constitutions, and neither government under that constitution nor society disintegrated during the war or postwar decade, as some of the conservatives had feared.

While the new state constitution provided the basis for social change, its framers were simply making legal what was already in the process of taking place or had earlier been demanded; that is, the Constitution of 1776 did not drastically alter North Carolina society. The process of democratization had already begun before the decision for independence had been made. While the lower voting and officeholding requirements and checks against multiple officeholding broadened the base of political participation, the regulator grievances had indicated that it was not so much voting restrictions that kept men from going to the polls as apathy and the manner in which elections were held. Part of the regulator purpose was to motivate people to elect responsible officials and to oust corrupt politicians. The constitutional provisions with respect to officeholding codified earlier regulator demands that would (hopefully) prevent corruption in government.

Many men from middling circumstances or obscure origins sat in the legislature during the 1780s (indicative of the broadened political base), but a number of assemblymen before 1776 had also come from "middling" circumstances (especially the representatives from the western counties). While political participation was extended, however, the "Better Sort" still provided the political leadership, not only for the conservatives but also for the radicals. The Eton-educated, stylish gentleman, Willie Jones, led the radicals (later Antifederalists) while his brother, Allen Jones, was one of the leading conservatives. The leaders of the radicals had been able to give up their elitist views — at least outwardly — and were willing to listen to and help mold public opinion. The people still recognized class lines but before the law all white men were equal. The large rural middle class in the state underscored that belief. In addition, both the ethnic diversity of the population, which promoted a toleration of various religious beliefs, and the ease by which one could climb the socioeconomic scale contributed to the leveling influence that had begun in colonial North Carolina. On the eve of the

Revolution many people (and no doubt some Anglicans among them) had believed that no one religious denomination should be given a privileged position in society. Even though the Church of England was established in the colony, in counties where the dissenters predominated, the church establishment had not been able to take root. Great Awakening doctrines, preached especially by the Baptists, also promoted the spirit of toleration and emphasized individual beliefs, which undermined the idea of a church establishment. The framers of the state constitution, then, disestablished the Church of England and made certain that no one religious denomination in the future would receive special privileges. Nevertheless, only Protestants could fully participate in politics; Catholics were barred from holding office. The doctrine of equality completely broke down, however, with respect to blacks. Although there was some antislavery sentiment in the new state, the institution continued, and in fact grew during the last two decades of the eighteenth century.

While the "Better Sort" in 1771 had been able to meet the challenge of the regulators and had effectively maintained their hold on politics, they soon after had to appeal to the masses (including many sympathetic to the regulator cause) for their support in the fight for independence. The revolutionary leaders then reiterated what regulator petitions or what Herman Husband had stated: that governors should be responsible to the people and should act in their best interest; that sovereignty lay with the people. North Carolinians in 1776 took their cue and demanded that their rights be protected and that power be granted to the people in the constitution. Once they had taken that power, however, they gave it back to the natural leaders, but not without due warning that public officials would now be scrupulously watched by the electorate.

The 1780s witnessed a continual political argument throughout the Confederation about the nature of government and the distribution of power. North Carolina was no exception. The revolutionary propaganda confirmed the farmer's belief in minimal government. While Thomas Jefferson wrote about the "noble agrarian" as the protector of republican values, the yeoman freeholders of North Carolina (where they held much more actual power than in Virginia) were practicing Jeffersonian theory. As the mercantile interests in the northeastern part of the state began to demand a stronger, more centralized national government, the old backcountry suspicions about governmental institutions and governors were aroused. The farmers viewed with distrust the new federal Constitution; they feared that too strong a central government would encroach upon their rights as individuals and would ultimately destroy republican government. On the other hand, the merchants feared the destruction of state and society and the subsequent rise of anarchy — sentiments similar to those expressed at the time of the regulator movement. Champions of the mercantile and agrarian views confronted each other in the ratification struggle over the federal

Constitution; a conflict that was in part interwoven with the issue of paper money as well as with the demand for a Bill of Rights. The Antifederalists, representing a large majority, believed that they were protecting republican government and the individual when they rejected the federal Constitution in 1788. Only after James Madison proposed amendments to the Constitution, and the Bill of Rights seemed a reality, did North Carolina ratify the document. The ratification struggle indicated the provincialism of the state, but it also illustrated the fear of government's encroachment upon the rights of the individual (which was, indeed, very much a possibility).

What did North Carolina, then, offer to the Revolution? The most prominent leaders in the revolutionary movement came from other colonies. The state could not rival Virginia or Massachusetts in revolutionary fervor. Many North Carolina citizens became loyalists or sat out the war. But the democratization of North Carolina society illustrated what the Revolution was all about. While American political theorists such as Jefferson wrote about the virtues of a republic of small farmers, North Carolina yeomen were giving credence to such remarks. Their values permeated North Carolina society. While Jefferson and other writers pushed for educational institutions in the young Republic, the North Carolina legislature incorporated eighteen academies and two "public" schools; more than any southern state before 1790. North Carolinians realized that the way to preserve republican government was through a literate citizenry. While the Antifederalists in other states failed, in North Carolina they succeeded in keeping the state out of the union until individual rights (as expressed in the first ten amendments) were protected.

North Carolina values became American values — before many North Carolinians fully realized that they themselves were American. North Carolinians continued to be provincial and to identify most readily with their local communities. But the outside world regarded them as American whether they did or not. The state represented a land of hope or opportunity for many individuals, where the industrious yeoman could indeed aspire to become a prosperous farmer; perhaps even a large planter. Only blacks, who contributed a great deal of labor, and Indians were left out of the picture of economic democracy. Just as the colony had stirred the imagination of Scottish Highlanders in 1770, so the state still projected the same image of economic opportunity in 1790. A cousin of Samuel Johnston's wrote to him from Edinburgh that year that more than a dozen men had applied for the position of gardener at Johnston's plantation: the majority "desparate" or "restive" who see "America as a Country where any could gather gold in the streets or fields."[2] North Carolinians were gradually becoming aware of the most fundamental change in their lives: that they were Americans, and not only their state but their country represented the pot of gold at the end of the rainbow for many individuals. But while they were slow to accept the fact because of their isolation which resulted in their provincial attitudes, they realized that they had taken part in the formation of a new government that was based on the will of the people. While the first families of other colonies are praised, North Carolina should be proud of those independent farmers who believed in individual rights — who, in essence, represented the idea of progress despite their provincialism — and who embodied the American Dream.

NOTES

CHAPTER I

¹Griffith J. McRee (ed.), *Life and Correspondence of James Iredell* (New York: Peter Smith [Reprint of 1857 ed.] 2 volumes, 1949), I, 116, 117, hereinafter cited as McRee, *Iredell.*

²A. R. Newsome (ed.), "Records of Emigrants from England and Scotland to North Carolina, 1774-1775," *North Carolina Historical Review,* XI (January, 1934), 130, hereinafter cited as Newsome, "Emigrant Records."

³"Information Concerning the Province of North Carolina, addressed to emigrants from the Highlands and Western Isles of Scotland, By an impartial hand," William K. Boyd (ed.), *Some Eighteenth Century Tracts Concerning North Carolina* (Raleigh: Edwards & Broughton Company, 1927), 438, hereinafter cited as Boyd, *Eighteenth Century Tracts.*

⁴Jackson Turner Main, *The Social Structure of Revolutionary America* (Princeton, New Jersey: Princeton University Press, 1965), 66, hereinafter cited as Main, *Social Structure.*

⁵William L. Saunders (ed.), *The Colonial Records of North Carolina* (Raleigh: State of North Carolina, 10 volumes, 1886-1890), VIII, 59, hereinafter cited as Saunders, *Colonial Records.*

⁶"A French Traveller in the Colonies, 1765," *American Historical Review,* XXVI (July, 1921), 738, hereinafter cited as "A French Traveller."

⁷"Autobiography of Col. William Few of Georgia," *Magazine of American History,* VII (July-December, 1881), 344, hereinafter cited as "Autobiography of Col. William Few"; Boyd, *Eighteenth Century Tracts,* 443, 446, 447.

⁸United States Bureau of the Census with the Cooperation of the Social Science Research Council, *The Statistical History of the United States from Colonial Times to the Present* (Stamford, Connecticut: Farifield Publishers, Inc., 1965), 756, hereinafter cited as U. S. Census, *Statistical History;* Saunders, *Colonial Records,* VII, 248; Boyd, *Eighteenth Century Tracts,* 446.

⁹Samuel Johnston to Robert Cathcart, November 8, 1774, folder 87, Hayes Collection, microfilm in the Southern Historical Collection, University of North Carolina, Chapel Hill, North Carolina, from originals in the possession of Mr. John G. Wood, Edenton, N. C.

¹⁰Robert W. Ramsay, *Carolina Cradle: Settlement of the Northwest Carolina Frontier, 1747-1762* (Chapel Hill: University of North Carolina Press, 1964), 20-25, hereinafter cited as Ramsay, *Carolina Cradle; North Carolina Magazine,* December 7-December 14, 1764, noted that some Marylanders came by ship instead of by wagon; Harry Roy Merrens, *Colonial North Carolina in the Eighteenth Century: A Study in Historical Geography* (Chapel Hill: University of North Carolina Press, 1964), 54-55, hereinafter cited as Merrens, *Colonial North Carolina;* Nannie M. Tilley, "The Settlement of Granville County," *North Carolina Historical Review,* XI (January, 1934), 14, hereinafter cited as Tilley, "Settlement of Granville County."

¹¹"Autobiography of Col. William Few," 343.

¹²Saunders, *Colonial Records,* VIII, 526; IX, 364; IV, 490, 599.

¹³Newsome, "Emigrant Records," 40, 130, 142.

¹⁴U. S. Census, *Statistical History,* 756.

¹⁵Charles W. Dunn (trans.), "Gaelic Poem Composed by John Macrae for his daughter," *North Carolina Historical Review,* XXXVI (October, 1959), 474, 475; Saunders, *Colonial Records,* IX, 364.

¹⁶Saunders, *Colonial Records,* VI, 431, 616; J. F. D. Smyth, *A Tour in the United States of America* (New York: Arno Press [Reprint of 1784 ed.], 2 volumes, 1968), I, 172, hereinafter cited as Smyth, *Tour in the United States;* Winslow C. Watson (ed.), *Men and Times of the Revolution or Memoirs of Elkanah Watson* (New York: Dana and Company, 1856), 294-296, hereinafter cited as Watson, *Men and Times of the Revolution.*

[17]U. S. Census, *Statistical History,* 756; Merrens, *Colonial North Carolina,* 75-77; Francis Grave Morris and Phyllis Mary Morris, "Economic Conditions in North Carolina About 1780: Part II. Ownership of Town Lots, Slaves, and Cattle," *North Carolina Historical Review,* XVI (July, 1939), 305, hereinafter cited as Morris, "Economic Conditions."

[18]Merrens, *Colonial North Carolina,* 197, 78-81.

[19]Saunders, *Colonial Records,* VI, 1027, 1028; *Commerce of Rhode Island 1726-1800,* 2 volumes, Massachusetts Historical Society, *Collections,* seventh series, IX (Boston, 1914), I, 489, 490, hereinafter cited as *Commerce of Rhode Island.*

[20]Saunders, *Colonial Records,* VI, 968; VII, 695-696; Adelaide L. Fries and others (eds.), *Records of the Moravians in North Carolina* (Raleigh: North Carolina Historical Commission [Office of Archives and History], 11 volumes, 1922-1969), I, 339, 356, 334, 400, hereinafter cited as Fries, *Moravian Records.*

[21]Harry J. Carman (ed.), *American Husbandry* (Port Washington, New York: Kennikat Press, Inc. [Reprint of 1939 ed.], 1964), 240, hereinafter cited as Carman, *American Husbandry;* "A French Traveller," 737.

[22]Charles Christopher Crittenden, *The Commerce of North Carolina 1763-1789* (New Haven: Yale University Press, 1936), 73, hereinafter cited as Crittenden, *Commerce of North Carolina;* Johann David Schoepf, *Travels in the Confederation, 1783-1784* (New York: Burt Franklin Reprint, 1968), 103, hereinafter cited as Schoepf, *Travels in the Confederation;* Merrens in *Colonial North Carolina,* 90, points out that Cumberland County had plenty of pine but slaves were unimportant and, thus, naval stores production was small.

[23]"A French Traveller," 733, 734, 738; Schoepf, *Travels in the Confederation,* 142.

[24]Schoepf, *Travels in the Confederation,* 73.

[25]Merrens, *Colonial North Carolina,* 96.

[26]Merrens, *Colonial North Carolina,* 95-98; Saunders, *Colonial Records,* VI, 1030; VII, 201, 202; Janet Schaw, *Journal of a Lady of Quality; Being the Narrative of a Journey from Scotland to the West Indies, North Carolina, and Portugal, in the years 1774-1776,* edited by Evangeline Walker Andrews with the collaboration of Charles McLean Andrews (New Haven: Yale University Press, 1923), 184, 185, hereinafter cited as Schaw, *Journal of a Lady of Quality;* "A French Traveller," 738.

[27]Crittenden, *Commerce of North Carolina,* 73; "A French Traveller," 738; *Commerce of Rhode Island,* I, 454; Saunders, *Colonial Records,* IX, 526; Hugh Buckner Johnston (ed.), "The Journal of Ebenezer Hazard in North Carolina, 1777 and 1778," *North Carolina Historical Review,* XXXVI (July, 1959), 365, hereinafter cited as Johnston, "Hazard." Merrens in *Colonial North Carolina,* 123, points out that while wheat and tobacco or corn and tobacco were grown together, farmers never cultivated wheat and corn at the same time.

[28]Schaw, *Journal of a Lady of Quality,* 159, 160, 163, 164.

[29]Schaw, *Journal of a Lady of Quality,* 152; "A French Traveller," 736; Schoepf, *Travels in the Confederation,* 108.

[30]Carman, *American Husbandry,* 240, 241; Morris, "Economic Conditions, Part II," 316-323.

[31]Alan D. Watson, "Society and Economy in Colonial Edgecombe County," *North Carolina Historical Review,* L (July, 1973), 251, 252, hereinafter cited as Watson, "Society and Economy in Colonial Edgecombe County."

[32]Saunders, *Colonial Records,* IX, 269; Schoepf, *Travels in the Confederation,* 108, 109.

[33]Crittenden, *Commerce of North Carolina,* 74; Merrens, *Colonial North Carolina,* 120-123; Morris, "Economic Conditions, Part II," 305.

[34]Watson, "Society and Economy in Colonial Edgecombe County," 245, 246; Carman, *American Husbandry,* 243.

[35]Saunders, *Colonial Records,* IX, 269, 364; Merrens, *Colonial North Carolina,* 127; *North Carolina Gazette,* November 15, 1755; August 29, 1777; April 3, 1778; June 13, 1778; July 10, 1778, November 30, 1778.

[36]Saunders, *Colonial Records,* VII, 489, 490; XXIII, 639-650, 728-741, 790, 948; Lida T. Rodman (ed.), *Journal of a Tour to North Carolina by William Attmore, 1787* (Chapel Hill: University of North Carolina Press [Volume 17 of the James Sprunt Historical Publications], 1922), 34-36, hereinafter cited as Rodman, *Attmore.* The latter journal gives a description of the inspection process.

[37]Saunders, *Colonial Records,* VI, 1027-1030; VII, 429, 430, 695, 696; VI, 1058, 1059; Walter

Clark (ed.), *The State Records of North Carolina* (Winston and Goldsboro: State of North Carolina, 16 volumes, numbered XI-XXVI, 1895-1907), XXIII, 613, hereinafter cited as Clark, *State Records.*

[38]Crittenden, *Commerce of North Carolina,* 74, 76.

[39]Crittenden, *Commerce of North Carolina,* 80-84; U. S. Census, *Statistical History,* 770.

[40]Crittenden, *Commerce of North Carolina,* 75, 78, 79, 105; Saunders, *Colonial Records,* VII, 429, 430.

[41]Hayes Collection, volume 14.

[42]Hayes Collection, volume 14; Crittenden, *Commerce in North Carolina,* 107.

[43]Virginia Bever Platt, "Tar, Staves and New England Rum: The Trade of Aaron Lopez of Newport, Rhode Island, with Colonial North Carolina," *North Carolina Historical Review,* XLVIII (January, 1971), 15-19.

[44]*Commerce of Rhode Island,* I, 384, 393.

[45]Smyth, *Tour in the United States,* I, 99; *North Carolina Gazette,* January 7, 1774; Nannie May Tilley, "Industries of Colonial Granville County," *North Carolina Historical Review,* XIII (October, 1936), 285.

[46]Johnston and Bennehan to Mr. John Alston, February 1, 1771, November 10, 1771, Cameron Family Papers, volume 5, Southern Historical Collection, University of North Carolina, Chapel Hill, N. C., hereinafter cited as Cameron Papers. Inventory figures are found in Volumes 3 and 4 of Cameron Papers. See also Marvin Lawrence Michael Kay, "The Institutional Background to the Regulation in Colonial North Carolina" (unpublished doctoral dissertation, University of Minnesota, 1962), hereinafter cited as Kay, "Institutional Background," 456, 479-482.

[47]Johnston and Bennehan to John Macfarlane and Company, July 12, 1784, Cameron Papers, volume 5; Johnston and Bennehan to Mr. John Nixon, January 10, 1772, Cameron Papers, volume 5.

[48]Merrens, *Colonial North Carolina,* 153; Crittenden, *Commerce of North Carolina,* 111.

[49]Crittenden, *Commerce of North Carolina,* 110; *Cape Fear Mercury,* September 22, 1773; Kay, "Institutional Background," 478, 479.

[50]Crittenden, *Commerce of North Carolina,* 100-102.

[51]Samuel Johnston to Thomas Barker, January 25, 1774, Hayes Collection, folder 80b.

[52]Samuel Johnston to Alexander Elmsley, June 10, 1771, Hayes Collection, folder 83.

[53]Saunders, *Colonial Records,* VII, 98, 99, 493, 494; VIII, 76, 77; William S. Powell, James K. Huhta and Thomas J. Farnham (eds.), *The Regulators in North Carolina* (Raleigh: North Carolina Department of Archives and History, 1971), 188, hereinafter cited as Powell, *Regulators in North Carolina;* Joseph Albert Ernst, *Money and Politics in America 1755-1775* (Chapel Hill: University of North Carolina Press [published for the Institute of Early American History and Culture], 1973), 199-207.

[54]Main, *Social Structure,* 66, 48, 49, 41-43.

[55]Field Book of Sundry Surveys, & Plans of Lands Belonging to Henry Eustace McCulloh, Southern Historical Collection, University of North Carolina, Chapel Hill, N. C.; Secretary of State, Lists of Land Grants By Counties, North Carolina Division of Archives and History, Raleigh, N. C.; Tilley, "Settlement of Granville County," 17; Smyth, *Tour in the United States,* I, 152. See also Merrens, *Colonial North Carolina,* 25, 26.

[56]Morris, "Economic Conditions, Part I," 120-129; Main, *Social Structure,* 53, 54; Jesse Forbes Pugh, *A Biographical History of Camden County* (Durham: Seeman Printing, Inc., 1957), 60.

[57]Main, *Social Structure,* 55; William S. Powell (ed.), "Tryon's 'Book' on North Carolina," *North Carolina Historical Review,* XXXIV (July, 1957), 411, hereinafter cited as Powell, "Tryon's 'Book' "; Merrens, *Colonial North Carolina,* 77, 130.

[58]Chowan County, List of Taxables, 1777, North Carolina Division of Archives and History, Raleigh, N. C., hereinafter cited as Chowan, Taxables, 1777. The figures for class divisions and conversion come from Main, *Social Structure,* 67, 161, 289.

[59]Chowan, Taxables, 1777; An Account of the taxable Estate of Samuel Johnston in Chowan County, 1777, Hayes Collection, folder 37; Samuel Johnston to John Ferrier, c. 1766, Hayes Collection, folder 60. For Virginia see Jackson Turner Main, "The One Hundred," *William and Mary Quarterly,* third series, XI (July, 1954), 354-384.

[60]William S. Price, " 'Men of Good Estates': Wealth among North Carolina's Royal

Councillors," *North Carolina Historical Review,* XLIX (January, 1972), 78, 79, hereinafter cited as Price, "Men of Good Estates."

⁶¹Schaw, *Journal of a Lady of Quality,* 297; Samuel Johnston to John Ferrier, c. 1766, Hayes Collection, folder 60.

⁶²Smyth, *Tour in the United States,* I, 161, 162.

CHAPTER II

¹Rowland Berthoff and John M. Murrin, "Feudalism, Communalism, and the Yeoman Free-holder: The American Revolution Considered as a Social Accident," in Stephen G. Kurtz and James H. Hutson (eds.) *Essays on the American Revolution* (Chapel Hill: University of North Carolina, 1973), 264, 276.

²Schaw, *Journal of a Lady of Quality,* 155.

³McRee, *Iredell,* I, 92, 93; *Commerce of Rhode Island,* I, 430.

⁴"Biographical Sketch of Waightstill Avery," *North Carolina University Magazine,* IV (August, 1855), 249, hereinafter cited as "Waightstill Avery," *University Magazine;* Samuel Johnston to Thomas Barker, February 8, 1770, Hayes Collection, folder 75; Schaw, *Journal of a Lady of Quality,* 156; McRee, *Iredell,* I, 126.

⁵McRee, *Iredell,* I, 126.

⁶William Price in "Men of Good Estates," 77, 79, takes issue with Jackson Turner Main's assertion in *The Upper House in Revolutionary America, 1763-1778* (Madison: University of Wisconsin, 1967), 21, hereinafter cited as Main, *Upper House in Revolutionary America,* that North Carolina's Council was dominated by placemen in the Revolutionary Era, but by his own evidence six placemen served on the council in the years 1763 to 1775. He misleads the reader by pointing out that eight of the twelve men that he designated placemen served before 1763, but two continued to serve in 1763 and after. I have thus added to the list: John Rutherfurd, whom Price admits could be called a placeman; and James Murray, who had become a prominent merchant by the 1760s, but had started out as a placeman.

⁷Samuel Johnston to Thomas Barker, August 20, 1766, Hayes Collection, folder 45.

⁸Nina Moore Tiffany (ed.), *Letters of James Murray, Loyalist* (Boston: Privately printed, 1901), 22, hereinafter cited as Tiffany, *Letters of James Murray.*

⁹Price, "Men of Good Estates," 79.

¹⁰Schaw, *Journal of a Lady of Quality,* 145.

¹¹Allen Johnson and Dumas Malone (eds.), *Dictionary of American Biography* (New York: Charles Scribner's Sons, 20 volumes, 1937), XV, 42; Ramsay, *Carolina Cradle,* 29, 26.

¹²Ramsay, *Carolina Cradle,* 112, 113.

¹³Powell, *Regulators in North Carolina,* 575, 579.

¹⁴Fries, *Moravian Records,* I, 251, 287; Ramsay, *Carolina Cradle,* 196; "Waightstill Avery," *University Magazine,* 254.

¹⁵Powell, *Regulators in North Carolina,* 60; Kay, "Institutional Background to the Regulators," 412, 422-424; Elisha P. Douglass, *Rebels and Democrats: The Struggle for Equal Political Rights and Majority Rule During the American Revolution* (Chapel Hill: University of North Carolina, 1955), 76.

¹⁶"Waightstill Avery," *University Magazine,* 254.

¹⁷Smyth, *Tour in the United States,* I, 114.

¹⁸Rodman, *Attmore,* 37, 38; Tiffany, *Letters of James Murray,* 22, 23; Schaw, *Journal of a Lady of Quality,* 153.

¹⁹"An Impartial Relation of the First Rise and Cause of the Present Differences in Public Affairs in the Province of North Carolina," Boyd, *Some Eighteenth Century Tracts,* 263, hereinafter cited as "Impartial Relation"; Saunders, *Colonial Records,* VII, 671, 672, 791, 792.

[20]Saunders, *Colonial Records,* VII, 884-886.

[21]Saunders, *Colonial Records,* VIII, 235; Powell, *Regulators in North Carolina,* 247, 252, 248; *Virginia Gazette,* October 25, 1770.

[22]Saunders, *Colonial Records,* VIII, 311, 312, 270, 481-486; Powell, *Regulators in North Carolina,* 327-329.

[23]Saunders, *Colonial Records,* VIII, 82.

[24]Saunders, *Colonial Records,* VIII, 76-78; "An Impartial Relation," Boyd, *Some Eighteenth Century Tracts,* 309; Saunders, *Colonial Records,* VIII, 195; IX, 49.

[25]"Fan for Fanning," Boyd, *Some Eighteenth Century Tracts,* 353.

[26]"An Impartial Relation," Boyd, *Some Eighteenth Century Tracts,* 302, 303.

[27]Karla Robinson, "The Regulation in Granville County, North Carolina" (unpublished seminar paper, University of North Carolina).

[28]Saunders, *Colonial Records,* IX, 329, 330.

[29]Powell, *Regulators in North Carolina,* 518, 519.

[30]Powell, *Regulators in North Carolina,* 526.

[31]McRee, *Iredell,* I, 335.

[32]McRee, *Iredell,* I, 338; *Constitution of the State of North Carolina,* 1776, Articles VII, VIII, V, VI, XXI, XXV, XXVII-XXX, XXXV, XXXIV.

[33]Main, *Upper House in Revolutionary America,* 154-158.

[34]Jackson Turner Main, *Political Parties Before the Constitution* (Chapel Hill: University of North Carolina Press, 1973), 312.

[35]McRee, *Iredell,* II, 41.

[36]Schoepf, *Travels in the Confederation,* 123, 124; Rodman, Attmore, 25.

[37]Rodman, *Attmore,* 16, 17.

[38]McRee, *Iredell,* II, 232.

[39]McRee, *Iredell,* II, 141.

CHAPTER III

[1]Quoted material is from Schoepf, *Travels in the Confederation,* 103; Johnston, "Hazard," 372; but impressions are based on the many travellers' accounts that have been previously cited.

[2]Watson, *Men and Times of the Revolution,* 289; Rodman, *Attmore,* 33.

[3]"A French Traveller," 736, 737; Rodman, *Attmore,* 41, 42.

[4]J. Fred Rippy, "A View of the Carolinas in 1783," *North Carolina Historical Review,* VI (October, 1929), 363, hereinafter cited as "A View of the Carolinas"; Smyth, *A Tour in the United States,* I, 103, 104.

[5]Frances Benjamin Johnston and Thomas Tileston Waterman, *The Early Architecture of North Carolina* (Chapel Hill: University of North Carolina Press, 1947), 34, hereinafter cited as Johnston and Waterman, *Early Architecture of North Carolina.*

[6]Rodman, *Attmore,* 45; Schoepf, *Travels in the Confederation,* 129; Johnston and Waterman, *Early Architecture of North Carolina,* 199.

[7]Johnston and Waterman, *Early Architecture of North Carolina,* 6, 7.

[8]Powell, " 'Tryon's Book'," 411; "Waightstill Avery," *University Magazine,* 252; Duane Meyer, *The Highland Scots of North Carolina, 1732-1776* (Chapel Hill: University of North Carolina Press, 1961), 126-128; Smyth, *A Tour in the United States,* I, 251.

[9]Schaw, *Journal of a Lady of Quality,* 185.

[10]Mary Haynes to Mrs. Waddell (or possibly Mrs. Burgwyn), August 19, 1764, Burgwyn Papers, folder 12, Southern Historical Collection, University of North Carolina, hereinafter cited as Burgwyn Papers.

[11]Powell, " 'Tryon's Book'," 411.

[12]Saunders, *Colonial Records,* IX, 239; "Autobiography of William Few," 343, 349.

[13]William K. Boyd (ed.) and Charles A. Krummel (trans.), "German Tracts Concerning the Lutheran Church in North Carolina during the Eighteenth Century. Part II. Velthusen's North Carolina Church Reports (I, II) with Ordination Address and Prayer," *North Carolina Historical Review,* VII (April, 1930), 245, hereinafter cited as Boyd, "German Tracts"; Alexander Elmsley to Samuel Johnston, April 7, 1775, folder 80b, Hayes Collection.

[14]Penelope Dawson to Samuel Johnston, c. 1773, folder 492, Hayes Collection; Penelope Dawson to Samuel Johnston, March 9, 1774, folder 87, Hayes Collection.

[15]"Autobiography of William Few," 344, 345, 352.

[16]Clark, *State Records,* XXV, 319-325; Onslow County, Apprentice Bonds, 1757-1907, Division of Archives and History, Raleigh; Rowan County, Apprentice Bonds, 1779-1891, Division of Archives and History, Raleigh; Edgecombe County, Guardian Accounts, Division of Archives and History, Raleigh.

[17]Samuel Johnston to Samuel Johnston, May 28, 1752, folder 32, Hayes Collection; Clark, *State Records,* XI, 722, 723.

[18]Saunders, *Colonial Records,* VI, 1048; Clark, *State Records,* XXV, 484, XXIII, 678-680.

[19]Saunders, *Colonial Records,* VI, 1048, VII, 104, IX, 238-243, 245-248; Thomas Thomlinson to the Reverend Dr. Burton, January 20, 1768, Society for the Propagation of the Gospel, Letters, Series B, 5, 13, 14, Microfilm in the Library at the University of California, Los Angeles.

[20]Clark, *State Records,* XXIII, 601-607; Saunders, *Colonial Records,* VIII, 486, 487.

[21]Henderson Letter Book, 1810-1811, Division of Archives and History, Raleigh, North Carolina.

[22]*North Carolina Magazine,* August 31-September 7, 1764.

[23]McRee, *Iredell,* I, 125.

[24]Schaw, *Journal of a Lady of Quality,* 155.

[25]"A View of the Carolinas in 1783," 363.

[26]James Iredell to Samuel Johnston, April 7, 1772, folder 84, Hayes Collection; McRee, *Iredell,* I, 132.

[27]Mary Burgwyn to Mrs. Waddell, 1769, folder 12, Burgwyn Papers; Disposition of Samuel Johnston, c. 1799, folder 486, Hayes Collection; Tiffany, *Letters of James Murray,* 116, 117.

[28]Boyd, "German Tracts," 245; Winthrop Jordan, *White Over Black: American Attitudes towards the Negro, 1550-1812* (Chapel Hill: University of North Carolina Press, published for the Institute of Early American History and Culture, 1968), 145.

[29]Schaw, *Journal of a Lady of Quality,* 161, 179.

[30]Penelope Dawson to Samuel Johnston, July 6, 1770, folder 70, Hayes Collection; Rodman, *Attmore,* 33; Ramsay, *Carolina Cradle,* 168, 169; *North Carolina Gazette,* January 9, 1778; 1774 indenture, folder 59, Hayes Collection.

[31]*South Carolina and American General Gazette,* February 9, 1776; Saunders, *Colonial Records,* X, 594; Watson, *Men and Times of the Revolution,* 287, 288.

[32]"Waightstill Avery," *University Magazine,* 248.

[33]McRee, *Iredell,* I, 379.

[34]Rodman, *Attmore,* 17, 18; McRee, *Iredell,* I, 514, 281, 282.

[35]Schaw, *Journal of a Lady of Quality,* 155; Schoepf, *Travels in the Confederation,* 117, 118, 148.

[36]Schaw, *Journal of a Lady of Quality,* 176, 177.

[37]Boyd, *Some Eighteenth Century Tracts,* 445.

[38]Penelope Dawson to Samuel Johnston, July 6, 1770, folder 70, Hayes Collection; Penelope Dawson to Samuel Johnston, December 17, 1774, folder 87, Hayes Collection.

[39]Schoepf, *Travels in the Confederation,* 147; Samuel Johnston to Nathaniel Duckenfield, June 30, 1786 or 1789, folder 102, Hayes Collection; Nathaniel Duckenfield to Samuel Johnston, November 21, 1786, folder 102, Hayes Collection.

[40]Alexander Stewart to Associates, August 12, 1762, American Correspondence, Dr. Bray's

Associates, photocopies in Library of Congress, hereinafter cited as Dr. Bray's Associates; Anthony Kinerin to the Reverend Alexander Stewart, January 21, 1764, American Correspondence, Dr. Bray's Associates; Alexander Stewart to Associates, May 7, 1764, Minute Book, September 6, 1764, Dr. Bray's Associates.

[41]Lewis De Rossett to Dr. Bray's Associates, April 22, 1765, Minute Book, October 3, 1765, Dr. Bray's Associates; John Barnett to the Associates, August 17, 1767, American Correspondence, Dr. Bray's Associates; Daniel Earl to the Associates, October 3, 1761, Minute Book, January, 1762, Dr. Bray's Associates.

[42]Saunders, *Colonial Records,* VI, 265; VII, 164; *North Carolina Gazette,* March 13, 1752.

[43]Clark, *State Records,* XXIII, 194-204; Donald R. Lennon and Ida Brooks Kellam (eds.), *The Wilmington Town Book, 1743-1778* (Raleigh: Division of Archives and History, 1973), 165-168, 209, 210; Schaw, *Journal of a Lady of Quality,* 199, 200.

[44]Rodman, *Attmore,* 38, 39.

[45]Saunders, *Colonial Records,* VI, 556, 236.

[46]Sarah McCulloh Lemmon, "The Genesis of the Protestant Episcopal Diocese of North Carolina, 1701-1823," *North Carolina Historical Review,* XXVIII (October, 1951), 436; Saunders, *Colonial Records,* VI, 1027; VII, 102; IX, 21, 22.

[47]Saunders, *Colonial Records,* VII, 102; VIII, 14, 15.

[48]Saunders, *Colonial Records,* VII, 241; VIII, 179, 202-210.

[49]Saunders, *Colonial Records,* XXIII, 853; VII, 541.

[50]George Washington Paschal, *History of North Carolina Baptists* (Raleigh: The General Board, North Carolina Baptist State Convention, 2 volumes, 1930), I, 264, hereinafter cited as Paschal, *North Carolina Baptists.*

[51]Paschal, *North Carolina Baptists,* I, 286, 287, 289.

[52]Paschal, *North Carolina Baptists,* I, 356, 148, 149; Saunders, *Colonial Records,* VI, 562.

[53]Saunders, *Colonial Records,* VI, 315; VII, 97; IX, 1003.

EPILOGUE

[1]Alice Barnwell Keith (ed.), *The John Gray Blount Papers* (Raleigh: Division of Archives and History, 3 vols., 1952), I, 8, 9.

[2]Robert Ferrier to Samuel Johnston, June 15, 1790, folder 127, Hayes Collection.

BIBLIOGRAPHIC NOTE

Primary Sources

In undertaking this study of North Carolina society I relied primarily upon printed sources and secondary works because of the time involved. But I did examine some manuscript materials that were very valuable for the view that they gave of North Carolina society; for example, the Hayes Collection, microfilm in the Southern Historical Collection, University of North Carolina Library, Chapel Hill, North Carolina, which contains correspondence, accounts, fee books, and indentures of Samuel Johnston and his family and provides a view of their lifestyle, and the Cameron Family Papers, which contain the correspondence of William Johnston and Richard Bennehan and the account books of their Snow Camp Store. The latter are useful for understanding the commercial transactions and the degree of prosperity of a country store in the Piedmont. The Robert Hogg Account Books, 1762-1775, illustrate the activities of a larger business firm, and the James Hogg Papers, 1772-1824, offer a glimpse of the reasons why Scottish Highlanders migrated and some of their difficulties. These manuscripts are also in the Southern Historical Collection.

The North Carolina Division of Archives and History possesses important materials for a study of North Carolina colonial and revolutionary society, which have not been fully utilized; for instance, the county records which include tax lists, estate records, guardian accounts, wills, and court proceedings. I barely scratched the surface; much more research needs to be done with these local materials.

Unfortunately for historians, few North Carolina newspapers survived the Revolutionary Era. Existent copies are on microfilm of *The Cape-Fear Mercury,* Wilmington, 1769-1775; *The North-Carolina Gazette,* New Bern, 1768-1778; *The North-Carolina Gazette,* Wilmington, 1765-1766; and *The North-Carolina Magazine; or Universal Intelligencer,* New Bern, 1764-1765. *The North-Carolina Gazette,* New Bern, resumed publication in 1783. *The Virginia Gazette* and *The South Carolina Gazette* both contain North Carolina material.

With respect to printed sources consulted, *The Colonial Records of North Carolina,* edited by William L. Saunders (Raleigh: State of North Carolina, 10 volumes, 1886-1890) and *The State Records of North Carolina,* edited by Walter Clark (Winston and Goldsboro: State of North Carolina, 16 volumes, 1895-1907), contain not only important legislative material and statutes but also letters to the Society for the Propagation of the Gospel and the correspondence of various public officials. Other useful documentary materials include Adelaide L. Fries and others (eds.), *Records of the Moravians in North Carolina* (Raleigh: North Carolina Historical Commission [Division of Archives and History], 11 volumes, 1922-1969), which provide not only a view of Moravian life in Wachovia but the Moravian view of their fellow North Carolinians; A. R. Newsome (ed.), "Records of Emigrants from England and Scotland to North Carolina, 1774-1775," *North Carolina Historical Review,* XI (January, 1934), in which the Highlanders cite the reasons why they want to migrate to North Carolina; and William S. Powell and others (eds.), *The Regulators in North Carolina* (Raleigh: North Carolina Division of Archives and History, 1971), which provides a comprehensive documentation for the regulator movement. The latter contains only excerpts from Herman Husband's accounts of the regulator movement, but his pamphlets are completely printed in William K. Boyd (ed.), *Some Eighteenth Century tracts Concerning North Carolina* (Raleigh: Edwards and Broughton Company, 1927). Boyd also includes the promotional literature written by Scotus Americanus.

In obtaining a contemporary (although sometimes biased) view of North Carolina society, travellers accounts, memoirs, and personal correspondence are invaluable. Janet Schaw's *Journal of a Lady of Quality; Being the Narrative of a Journey from Scotland to the West Indies, North Carolina, and Portugal, in the Years 1774 to 1776,* edited by Evangeline Walker Andrews (New Haven: Yale University Press, 1923), is an especially lively account. Other informative journals and personal papers especially useful were: "A French Traveller in the Colonies, 1765," *American Historical Review,* XXVI (July, 1921); "Autobiography of Col. William Few of Georgia," *Magazine of American History,* VII (July-December, 1881); Griffith J. McRee (ed.), *Life and Correspondence of James Iredell* (New York: Peter Smith [Reprint of 1857 ed.] 2 volumes, 1949); Lida T. Rodman (ed.), *Journal of a Tour to North Carolina by William Attmore, 1787* (Chapel Hill: University of North Carolina Press [Volume 17 of the James Sprunt Publications], 1922); Johann David Schoepf, *Travels in the Confederation, 1783-1784* (New York: Burt Franklin Reprint, 1968); and J. F. D. Smyth, *A Tour in the United States of America* (New York: Arno Press [Reprint of 1784 ed.] 2 volumes, 1968).

Secondary Sources
In examining the economic and demographic factors in Revolutionary North Carolina, Harry Roy Merrens's study, *Colonial North Carolina in the Eighteenth Century: A Study in Historical Geography* (Chapel Hill: University of North Carolina Press, 1964) was invaluable. Charles C. Crittenden, *The Commerce of North Carolina, 1763-1789* (New Haven: Yale University Press, 1936) and Francis Grave Morris and Phyllis Mary Morris, "Economic Conditions in North Carolina About 1780, Part I, Landholdings," *North Carolina Historical Review,* XVI (April, 1939), 107-133, and "Part II, Ownership of Town Lots, Slaves, and Cattle," *North Carolina Historical Review,*

XVI (July, 1939), 296-327, also provided useful information. More local history needs to be written, but an especially helpful monograph concerned with Rowan County was Robert W. Ramsay, *Carolina Cradle: Settlement of the Northwest Carolina Frontier, 1747-1762* (Chapel Hill: University of North Carolina Press, 1964). Another noteworthy local study is Alan D. Watson, "Society and Economy in Colonial Edgecombe County," *North Carolina Historical Review*, L (July, 1973), 231-255.

To understand the social structure of colonial North Carolina and put it in the context of other colonies, Jackson Turner Main's books, *The Social Structure of Revolutionary America* (Princeton: Princeton University Press, 1965) and *The Upper House in Revolutionary America, 1763-1778* (Madison: University of Wisconsin Press, 1967), proved especially useful. William S. Price, " 'Men of Good Estates': Wealth Among North Carolina's Royal Councillors," *North Carolina Historical Review*, XLIX (January, 1972), 72-82, disagrees with some of Main's conclusions and gives some interesting data. One recent study on the regulators should be mentioned: Marvin Lawrence Michael Kay's dissertation, "The Institutional Background to the Regulation in Colonial North Carolina," University of Minnesota, 1962.

The most useful book for North Carolina architecture is Frances Benjamin Johnston and Thomas Tileston Waterman, *The Early Architecture of North Carolina* (Chapel Hill: University of North Carolina Press, 1947). Other secondary works consulted especially for chapter three included studies on religion and slavery. Sarah McCulloh Lemmon, "The Genesis of the Protestant Episcopal Diocese of North Carolina, 1701-1823," *North Carolina Historical Review*, XXVIII (October, 1951), 426-462, discusses the problems of the Church of England in North Carolina and should be noted. One of the most comprehensive of the various religious histories on North Carolina is George Washington Paschal, *History of North Carolina Baptists*, Vol. I (Raleigh: The General Board, North Carolina Baptist State Convention, 2 volumes, 1930), which proved invaluable for an understanding of the activities of the Baptists in this period.

Slavery in eighteenth-century North Carolina needs further study. Most works are concerned with the antebellum South. Two older works that were somewhat useful were Rosser Howard Taylor, *Slaveholding in North Carolina: An Economic View* (Chapel Hill: University of North Carolina Press [Volume 15 of the James Sprunt Publications], 1926) and John S. Bassett, *Slavery and Servitude in North Carolina* (Baltimore: Johns Hopkins University [Volumes IV and V, Fourteenth Series, of the Johns Hopkins University Studies in Historical and Political Science], 1896). Winthrop D. Jordan, in *White Over Black* (Chapel Hill: University of North Carolina Press, published for the Institute of Early American History and Culture, 1968) covers racial attitudes in North Carolina and offers a comparison with other colonies.

There is little doubt that more work can and should be undertaken for a better understanding of North Carolina society before 1790.